—The Call of the Sea—

H.M.S. ELECTRA
ROYAL FLEET RESERVE

The Call of the Sea

Britain's Maritime Past 1900–1960

• Steve Humphries •

BBC BOOKS

Page 2: **Sailors report for duty at the naval barracks in Chatham, September 1939. At the beginning of the war Britain was thought to have the most powerful navy in the world.**

Overleaf: **Wild storms in the North Sea.**

This book is published to accompany the television series, entitled *The Call of the Sea*, made for the BBC by Testimony Films.
Executive producer: Sam Organ
Producer: Steve Humphries

Published by BBC Books
an imprint of BBC Worldwide Publishing
BBC Worldwide Limited, Woodlands,
80 Wood Lane, London W12 0TT

First published 1997

ISBN: 0-563-38722-X

Additional research by Steve Grogan and Sally Mullen

Designed by Andrew Shoolbred

Printed and bound in Great Britain by Butler and Tanner Limited,
Frome and London
Jacket printed by Lawrence Allen Limited,
Weston-super-Mare

Contents

Acknowledgements

Many people have made this book and the television series it accompanies possible. Thanks most of all to Sam Organ of BBC Bristol who first had the idea for a television history of maritime Britain. Thanks also to the team who worked on the series and helped to find the interviewees quoted – Martyn Ives, Richard Van Emden and Sharon Tanton. And thanks to everyone at BBC Books – Sheila Ableman, Anna Ottewill, Frank Phillips and Andrew Shoolbred for their work on the book.

Thanks also to Daniel de Waal, Andy Attenburrow, Steve Haskett, Jeff John, Jan Faull and the staff of the National Film and Television Archive, the staff of the BBC Bristol Reference Library, Madge Reed, Mike Humphries, Paul Thompson, Rob Perks, Mary Parsons, the staff of the National Maritime Museum in Portsmouth, Tony Carew, The Northern Lighthouse Board, Trinity House, Alec Gill, The Imperial War Museum, Stephen and Olive Peet, Nick Moss, Marika Sherwood, Sue Denny and the staff of the RNLI Press Office and Library, Charles Small, Bruce Batten, William and Arthur Badcock, Roy Bryant, Peter Durnford, Flora Murray, Ted and Laura Rillatt, Kay Needham-Hurst, Tony Lane, Sheila Jemima, Donny Hislop, Alan Scarfe, Melissa Pratt, Pat and Colin Grogan, Royal Navy Association and the Fleet Air Arm Museum.

Finally, thanks to all those old seafarers who told us their stories.

Introduction

For the generation that was brought up before the Second World War there was absolutely no doubt that Britain was the greatest seafaring nation in the world. This was the era when our Royal Navy, merchant fleet and fishing industry were second to none. Britain's naval supremacy went virtually unchallenged and seafaring provided a way of life for more than a million men and women.

This book, and the television series it accompanies, tells the story of the romance, the drama and the eventual decline of Britain's seapower in the first half of the century. It chronicles some of the lost skills of the oldest surviving generation who went to sea. This was an age when a skipper went deep-sea fishing without the aid of radar or radio, when Scots herring girls were famous for their extraordinary ability to gut thirty or forty fish a minute and when deck hands on the trawlers would work for days without sleep in the roughest seas.

The darker, more secret side of Britain's maritime past is also explored. Prostitutes in Shanghai, seedy night clubs in Buenos Aires and the promise of a woman in every port were all part of the allure of a life at sea. Despite the fact

Right: **A seaman's view of a convoy passing through the North Sea in 1943. During the Second World War Britain was dependent upon these merchant convoys, which carried essential supplies.**

Overleaf: **London's busy King George V Dock in 1938. Before the last war, Britain possessed the largest merchant fleet in the world.**

EAST FERRY
3
TONS

that the Navy tried to instil a spirit of obedience in sailors, there was considerable resistance to authority. Pilfering of cargoes and food, sabotage and jumping ship to escape from harsh conditions were all commonplace. There were more than fifty mutinies in the Royal Navy alone during the first half of this century, most of them provoked by injustice, incompetence or the often appalling conditions on the lower decks.

A seafaring life was the most dangerous that anyone could choose. Several hundred men were lost on British ships each year during the first decades of the century. Dramatic stories of shipwreck, survival and rescue are all part of our maritime tradition. Up to the 1930s the lifeboat service still predominantly used rowing and sailing boats to rescue the crews of ships in distress, which could make the task of the early RNLI volunteers hazardous indeed.

Since the Second World War, however, Britain has lost much of its old sea power. The Royal Navy, the merchant fleet and the fishing industry are all a shadow of their former selves. This decline was in fact deep-rooted and evident long before the 1950s. During the inter-war years there was an unemployment rate of around 20 per cent among merchant seamen, reflecting the diminishing size of Britain's merchant fleet. In bad years some fishing communities were reduced to the breadline. And even the Royal Navy was not the invincible force it had once been. During the last war it suffered heavy losses and, until 1942, was undoubtedly losing the war at sea.

The dramatic changes that have occurred in Britain's maritime activities make the recording of the memories of those who worked at sea all the more important. The world they knew has changed beyond recognition and will soon slip from living recall. In writing this book around 2000 people born between the 1890s and the 1940s have been interviewed or corresponded with. By drawing on this wealth of original material the book aims to provide a fresh and vivid account of seafaring Britain. Each chapter explores an important theme in our maritime history. Some, like those on mutiny and women, consider areas that have been largely overlooked by historians. All open with an introductory overview that sets the background to the personal reminiscences that follow, which form the larger part of the book. The voices we hear are those of about forty people who were filmed for the television series and were interviewed in depth. Through their stories we can begin to understand what 'the call of the sea' meant to the generations who were brought up before the Second World War.

— 1 —

Oceans Apart

The call of the sea meant to many young men the promise of romantic adventure. The life of a sailor, voyaging around the world, offered a freedom and excitement that held a special appeal for those brought up when Britain was the foremost seafaring nation in the world. Jolly Jack Tar, as the sailor used to be known, was a folk hero, reputed to have a different woman in every port. It was part myth it gave prestige and glamour to a job that was often low-paid and monotonous – but there was a reality, too, which inspired many a young man to pack his bags and join the Royal Navy or the merchant fleet in search of adventure. Yet, if distance from home and family brought glamour to life at sea, it could also bring loneliness and heartache. The long separation of seafarers from their girlfriends, wives and children made relationships at home difficult to maintain. Ultimately there was often a painful choice to be made between their family and their love of the sea.

Many boys brought up in the first half of the century dreamed of a life at sea. The Royal Navy, with its proud tradition of invincibility on the high seas, was much celebrated as the cornerstone of the British Empire. Its glorious role defending an island nation and policing the world – dispatching gunboats to settle disputes on distant shores – was part of the folklore of Empire. In the early 1920s there were 133,000 men in the Royal Navy, a figure that was to rise dramatically to almost 300,000 at the beginning of the Second World War. A host of naval training establishments prepared boys for the 'senior service', the most prestigious of all being Dartmouth Royal Naval College, in Devon, for officer

ROYAL NAVY
STOKERS
REQUIRED
NO PREVIOUS EXPERIENCE NECESSARY
Age: 18 to 25 years
CONTINUOUS SERVICE
12 YEARS IN THE FLEET
SPECIAL SERVICE
5 YEARS IN THE FLEET FOLLOWED BY SERVICE IN THE RESERVE TO COMPLETE 12 YEARS FROM DATE OF ENTRY
FREE KIT AND BEDDING ON ENTRY
FREE BOARD AND LODGING
GOOD PAY; GOOD PROSPECTS FOR MEN DESIROUS OF GETTING ON
EXTRA PAY FOR GOOD CONDUCT BADGES AND FOR SPECIAL DUTIES
For further particulars see special Handbook, "How to Join the Royal Navy," which can be obtained at any Post Office, or from:
Man on joining receives, if entered for 5 years 9/11
If entered for 12 years 11/8 per week
AT THE DEPOT
MAKING AND MENDING CLOTHES
FIRST CLASS
/7 to 16/4 per week
RECREATION
LEADING STOKER
18/8 to 19/10 per week
IN THE MEDITERRANEAN
STOKER-PETTY OFFICER
22/2 to 24/6 per week
GOING ON LEAVE
CHIEF STOKER
26/10 to 40/10 per week
WARRANT MECHANICIAN
£136 to £191 per year
MECHANICIAN
31/6 to 45/6 per week
ON THE CHINA STATION
(COPYRIGHT)

cadets. Here the gung-ho spirit of naval adventure ran so deep that the boys were taught that Britain had never lost a major sea battle in its entire history.

Most boys who went to sea, though, began on fishing and cargo boats. Before the Second World War Britain possessed a fishing fleet larger than any other. Its merchant fleet carried almost half of the world's shipping, providing jobs for more than 100,000 merchant seamen. The ships operating from the big fishing ports like Grimsby and Lowestoft and the great cargo ports like Liverpool, London and Cardiff could fire the imagination of children growing up nearby – as George Field from Wandsworth and George Rushmer from Lowestoft remember. They offered the promise of travel to exciting destinations all over Britain and the world in an age, before the package holiday, when few working-class families left their home town.

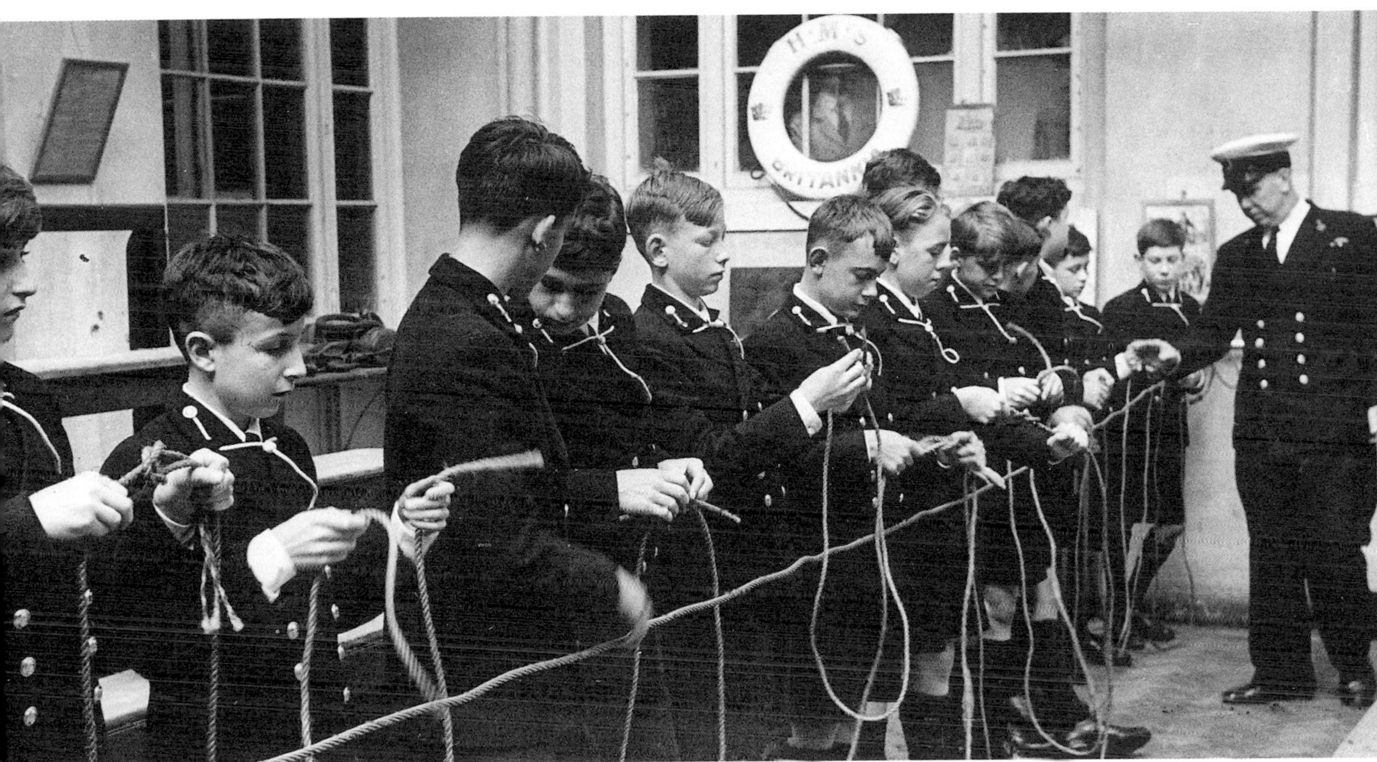

Left: **A Royal Navy recruiting poster for stokers in the First World War. The image of the adventurous sailor travelling the globe inspired many young men to go to sea.**

Above: **Boy cadets under instruction at Dartmouth in the 1940s. The belief that Britain was an invincible naval power was instilled into future officers.**

Britain also boasted a tradition of amateur sailors, lured by the romance and challenge of the sea, keen to battle with the elements. A few were attracted to the old sailing ships, which, by the 1930s, had been largely superseded by steam and diesel. One of the most extraordinary adventurers was Adrian Seligman, who bought an old three-masted schooner, the *Cap Pilar*, with a legacy left to him by his grandfather and set off in 1936 on a voyage for the South Sea Islands together with a novice crew.

The reality of life at sea was, for the raw recruits, often very different from what they expected. Merchant seamen had to endure working and living conditions that harked back to Victorian times. Similarly, the harsh discipline of the Royal Navy could come as a shock for the newcomer and was a frequent cause of resentment on the lower deck. Some deserted and never went to sea again, but most stuck it out. For, despite all the hardships, they were attracted by the freedom and adventure offered by the sea. As many old seafarers we spoke to put it, the sea 'got into their blood'.

The remembered pleasures of the sea we have collected are many and varied – the skills of navigation and seamanship, travelling to faraway places, the challenge of sailing in adverse weather and conditions. The appeal of a life at sea mirrored the sharp divisions between the upper and lower deck. For officers, service in the Royal Navy in peacetime could sometimes be dominated by an endless round of pleasurable social events. Captain Mervyn Wingfield, posted to the Far East in the 1930s, wryly recalls that the lifestyle of the officers was virtually one of 'subsidized yachting'.

In contrast, harsh, physical work on the lower deck fostered strong bonds of comradeship among the ratings. Working in the close confines of the ship encouraged a fierce tribal identity, which was heightened by the frustrations that built up during a long voyage at sea. Seamen in port were proud of their tough, hard drinking and their macho reputation which, when challenged, could quickly explode into violence. The fights that resulted were part of the excitement of a life at sea. They were usually between British and foreign sailors or between British sailors from different ships – the greatest rivalry being between crews from London and Liverpool. Fighting to protect their honour in foreign bars – which might occasionally turn into a riot – was a proud tradition of the merchant seaman. Bill Hart, from Liverpool, was a merchant seaman between the 1930s and the 1950s.

Climbing the top mast of a sailing ship. Steam and diesel had largely taken over by the 1930s but for many the allure of vessels like these was still powerful.

'The Liverpool seamen were always on edge with London seamen... they thought they acted in a slightly superior way, and, if there was a conflict, it was usually between the Liverpool and the London crowd. But if the locals caused the problem there was a unity of purpose – you'd all be united against the common enemy whoever they might be. I remember one particular battle I was involved in. It started in a cafe in Montreal by the Place Vichy Hotel, and to begin with the battle was between the Liverpool and London seamen, and all the tables were being smashed up and it spilled into the street. Then the French-Canadian police waded in, so now it's a battle of all of us against the Montreal police. In the end they had to get the whole of the Montreal police force out and they were lined up on one side of the road, we were on the other, and we knocked hell out of them, we drove them across the road and into a public park. They retreated because the seamen's dander was really up. Anyway, that went down in seamen's folklore – amongst seamen the battle of Place Vichy was known all over the world.'

The greatest adventure of all offered by a life at sea was sexual. This was reflected in the lasting reputation of the British seafarer as a womanizer, sowing his wild oats in every port of call the world over. Frustrated by weeks or months spent solely in the company of men and often a long way from home, his main preoccupation was with sexual pleasure – which frequently had to be bought. Around the waterfront there were 'sailor towns' – much the same the world over whether in London, Buenos Aires or Shanghai – to service the men's most basic needs and relieve them of their pay. The seafarer probably enjoyed greater sexual freedom and opportunity than almost any other occupation in Britain during the first half of the twentieth century.

Sexual experience with women and sexual conquests were regarded as proof of manhood in this tough, masculine world. As many were ignorant about sex and there was still a widespread taboo on sex before marriage, prostitutes played an important role in the sexual initiation of many young seamen. They were often aided and abetted by older crew members in what was essentially a rite of passage into adulthood and acceptance as a fully fledged seafarer. Tom Gooding, who served in the Royal Navy's Far East Fleet in the 1930s, had sex for the first time with a Japanese prostitute... assisted by his Master at Arms.

'She was on this wooden bed in the prone position and the Master at Arms pointed to that particular part of her anatomy and he said "Well, there you are boy". And I didn't have a clue so he just grabbed hold of me by the back of the

Merchant seamen at work in the late 1940s.

neck, forced me down on top of this young lady. He said "Come on, get moving", and he literally put it where it should go. Even then I wasn't doing what he thought I should do and he said "Come on boy for God's sake!" and he smacked me on the bottom... and things began to move and suddenly there was a thundering rush of blood to my ears and it was over.'

Sex for sale remained high on the list of priorities for many men as soon as they arrived in port. A few sailor towns achieved world renown among seamen for the erotic delights on offer. Before the First World War San Francisco was the most cherished destination for the seafarer looking for sexual adventure. The waterfront area known as 'The Barbary Coast' was a vast array of dance halls filled with friendly hostesses and dancers whose main income was from prostitution. In the year 1900 alone over a thousand British seamen deserted in 'Frisco. During the inter-war years San Francisco was cleaned up and Far Eastern ports like Yokohama and Shanghai became very popular. Rickshaw 'coolies' operating on the quayside were often paid by brothel owners to bring visiting seamen direct to their premises. But perhaps more than anywhere else Buenos Aires was the mecca for commercial sex during the inter-war years. In the 1930s there were an estimated 25,000 prostitutes working in the Argentinian capital: the cheapest walked the streets, while the more expensive were based in the bordellos, nightclubs, cabaret joints and dance halls that hugged the waterfront. One seaman who made regular trips to the red-light district in Buenos Aires was John Cockle from Truro, Cornwall, who remembers it was a 'sailor's paradise'.

The main British ports – especially London, Liverpool, Cardiff and Plymouth – had long been centres of prostitution. In 1926 one official report, 'The Protection of the Health of Seamen Against Venereal Disease', claimed that in British ports 'there are houses of ill fame everywhere in the seamen's quarters and loose women swarm in all the streets'. Tiger Bay in the dockland area of Butetown, Cardiff, was fairly typical of this kind of red-light district. Alongside the shipping offices, the ship's chandlers and the warehouses there were all night cafés, pubs, clubs, brothels, illegal drinking establishments and opium dens, most of which had prostitutes attached to them. Although soliciting for sex was illegal in Britain – as it was in most other countries – the police often turned a

Left: **Two naval reservists arrive at Portsmouth to join their ships.**

Overleaf: **British sailors on shore leave in the South of France in 1937. Frustrated by weeks or months at sea most eventually found their way to the seedy bars of 'sailortown'.**

TABACS

CAFÉ DE

Merchant seamen enjoying female company in London in 1942. Seaman's missions arranged social events to encourage abstinence and respectability.

blind eye to this in what was a complex web of control and corruption.

The roving life of the seafarer was well suited to the single, young man with no attachments. When love and marriage arrived all this would change. The men who went to sea had seen the world and so were glamorous and romantic figures to many young women looking for a marriage partner. But when they married many men would feel increasingly torn between their life at home and their life at sea. This dilemma was heightened by the growing popularity of marriage and family life among seafarers. In the days of sail it was predominantly single men who worked at sea, but, as steam reduced journey times and made voyages more predictable, family life was brought more within the grasp of the seafarer. In an era which celebrated the ideal of the happy family with father as provider, the itinerant nature of work at sea encouraged men to put down roots on shore and set up home. By the 1930s most seafaring men were married by the time they reached their mid-twenties or thirties.

Combining a career at sea with marriage and family life had never presented too much of a problem to the officer class. They often enjoyed married quarters or, like Captain Wingfield, had the means to take their wife with them wherever they were posted. The great majority of married men working at sea, however, did not have their wives by their side and saw little of them. Some, like John Cockle, continued to relish the prospect of a different woman in every port. But most found it very difficult to juggle the conflicting demands of work and family. The long separation from home was very painful. The adventure of voyages that had been so appealing to the young now began to be a serious problem.

Deep-sea trawlermen or fishermen following the herring were away from home for several weeks and would only be home for a couple of days before they had to go back to sea again. Merchant seamen could be away from home for many months on long trips and, before the Second World War, ratings in the Royal Navy had to work two and a half years for every month's leave.

When children arrived it could become even more difficult. Many seafaring fathers were abroad when their babies were born and they saw precious little of them as they grew up. Mothers tended to bring up the children virtually single-handed. This separation put an enormous strain on a husband's relationship with his wife and on a father's relationship with his children. Despite the much looked forward to homecoming and the ritual present-giving, most men were virtual strangers to their sons and daughters. Sid Graham was a stoker on cargo boats operating from London between the 1930s and the 1950s.

'You really looked forward to coming home to see your wife and your children… it's like being born again when you come home, everything's lovey-dovey.

I'd be shovelling the coal in that furnace, couldn't put it in fast enough to get home, and I'd always bring them presents – bring them monkeys, canaries, parrots, dolls for the girls – they'd always expect something and they'd run up to me and hug me. When I left I used to kiss the kids, but I wouldn't let them see me to the door – just walk away, otherwise you get real melancholy. It's a terrible feeling when you're leaving, you feel downhearted.'

Low wages and unemployment put an added pressure on family life in the fishing ports and seaports. The fishing industry was in decline and the slump in world trade in the 1920s and 1930s meant that there was less demand for the labour of merchant seamen. Their unemployment rate remained high – around 20 per cent throughout the inter-war years. There might be weeks, months or, in a few cases, years of unemployment between voyages, and few shipowners paid retainers to men even though they might have devoted their working life to a shipping company. The slump also kept wages down in both the merchant fleet and the Royal Navy. Worst off in the Royal Navy were able seamen who had married young, for no marriage allowance was paid to those under 25. Out of a total basic pay of one pound three shillings (£1.15) he had to support himself as well as a wife and, possibly, a family at home. The combined pressure of poverty and separation was too much for some couples. In an age before divorce was socially acceptable a few husbands went to sea never to return.

As the family commitments of the seafarer grew, so too did the pressure on him to give up his life at sea. The conflict between the pull of the sea and the even stronger pull of family life was too much to bear for many fathers. They resolved it by taking shore jobs, as did Sid Graham in 1960 after he discovered that the long separation from his eldest daughter Esther was making her very ill: 'The doctor told me she was pining so much she wasn't eating; he said she might die, so that settled me and I just gave it up there and then'.

Left: **Taking advantage of a brief period ashore in the late 1950s. The promise of a woman in every port was part of the enduring appeal of a life at sea.**

Above: **Families wave goodbye to their men at Portsmouth Naval Base. The enforced separation experienced by many sailors of the Royal Navy and Merchant fleet placed a great strain on family life.**

Sid – then 40 – was one of large numbers of men who were leaving the fishing and merchant fleet and the Royal Navy in their thirties and forties, to be replaced by younger men. But many of those who gave up the sea still vividly remember how hard it was to do so. Like George Field, they had to suppress a constant yearning for their old life which, despite all its hardships, had once given them a freedom and adventure that most found impossible to recapture.

GEORGE RUSHMER

George had an infectious enthusiasm for life. He lived in his home town of Lowestoft, Suffolk, with his wife Edie. A much loved local character, it took him a long time to walk through the town centre because of all the people who stopped him to say hello. George went to sea for eighteen years. He began on the herring boats and also had spells in the Royal Navy and the merchant fleet until 1953, when he decided to 'swallow the anchor' and began working ashore at the newly opened Birds Eye processing factory in Lowestoft. George and Edie have two daughters and four grandchildren. George died in September 1996.

Well, it's the great unknown, isn't it. It's adventure. And everything about fishing is physical, and I was really a physical boy – into all sorts of sports. And I just knew that I had to go to sea. I was raised amongst boats, loved playing in boats. But my father had advised me not to, with his experience at sea and him growing up and not knowing his family, so I stayed ashore till I was 17. Then I ran away. I tried to walk a hundred and fifty miles [240 kilometres] to Grimsby to get a ship. I didn't make it, but Father realized then when I got home that he couldn't stop me and he got me my first berth.

I'd never really been out of Lowestoft. My horizons were just the north beach, the south beach, and Lowestoft was a small place. So the great thing about the fishing was it gave me the chance to travel. So I started my first ship and I went round to Milford Haven in Wales – and that was a long way away, all the way down the English Channel, round Land's End, up the Irish Sea into Milford Haven. That took three days and that was my first journey in a ship. All new, and everything was great. And from Milford Haven we followed the herrings up to Stornoway, from Stornoway we went up to Lerwick – which is a great adventure, over a thousand drifters up there and we were up there for about six weeks. From Lerwick we came down to Peterhead, and down the coast stopping on the way to Scarborough – got to Scarborough just about the beginning of August. All the holiday-makers were there. That was terrific – they were there looking at us, they made us all feel like heroes, all wanted to come aboard the ship, didn't they. Now that was my first voyage, taking in all about 14 weeks, and I had been to all those places and seen all the coast of Britain, knew all the lighthouses and the lightships, everything that happened, all the sea life.

Marvellous! And my mates that worked ashore hadn't been out of Lowestoft, had they; they'd been going to their daily job, eight to five, weekends playing football, and that was it. Now I'd been to all them places and that was very exciting.

George and Edie Rushmer on their wedding day in 1944. George's marriage marked the end of his 'love affair with the sea' – now he wanted to come ashore and raise a family.

Well, for the first time in your life you are at sea and you can't see any land... you've got the horizon all round you. And the sea changes almost every hour and everything is different. You start off the day and there'll be a heavy, dark cloud, you won't see the sun come up and then all at once there'd be a break in the clouds, then there'll be a storm come along. Then the sea will change – one minute it's flat calm, the next minute it's chucking spray over the wheelhouse and you've got to take it on, ain't you, 'cos life is not easy in a drifter in a gale of wind I can assure you. And it can try your nerve, too, because you can see the bows of a drifter go into a wave and for a second or two you don't know whether you're going to come up or not – and I'm not exaggerating. And to me that's adventure. And then when you've been through a gale of wind and you tie up in the harbour, you have a real sense of achievement. Honestly, you think 'that's one to me', that is. And that's every trip.

Every day was an adventure... and then there was the independence. You were your own man, and as long as you did your job on board the ship, what you did when you got ashore was entirely up to you. Every few weeks somewhere new. Different scenery, different people, met a lot of people... and I took to it naturally. Well, it's all a challenge, and I know that fishermen can be quite profane when they like, can't they; it's a man's world, and what you say out there nobody else hears, but we would curse the wind and fight the wind, you know what I mean? She would try and get you down and you'd never let her beat you. Then there was the uncertainty – not knowing whether you're going to catch any fish or not. Every night when you went to haul the nets there was a big expectancy. Is there any fish there or isn't there, you know, and if there was fish you knew you was in for hours and hours of work. But I really did like the physical side. Everything you did was with your hands and your legs, and very primitive clothing – our protective clothing was really primitive. We used to be soaked to the skin in no time, carry on regardless, and very often you couldn't get them dry again till the next haul. And every time she rolled and took in sea we used to swear and get ready for the next one. Oh yeah, I loved it!

Well, my life changed completely during the war. I was in the Navy then, and I met my wife to be. It was like a thunderbolt. I cannot put into words the feeling that I felt when I first looked at her in that pub, in Grimsby docks. Boy oh boy she was gorgeous, she really was, and from that moment onwards my life changed. 'Cos she became a bloody nuisance, didn't she, because up until that time I was in love with the sea – the sea was all I wanted – and ships, but from the moment I met her I don't think I would have cared much if I'd have never left Grimsby then, I'm sure I wouldn't.

Well, Edie, she was a very attractive young girl, she was about eighteen years old, just the apple of my eye; and I'd had girlfriends, that wasn't my first occasion, but there was something there, an instant exchange of feelings. Really, as solid as that. The first night we went out we just could not leave each other, we went walking arm in arm. The problem was she was engaged to be married to another sailor and she'd been up to his house and met his parents. But she wanted to be with me, so when I took her back home there was hell to pay and mother-in-law was livid – with her for being out with me and her sailor was away at sea. But there's an old tradition with sailors, you know: if you want to get in anywhere, throw your hat in first, right. So Edie opened the front door with great trepidation. She knew she was in for a telling off and I didn't know what was going to happen to me, and she said 'Throw your hat in'. When the front door opened – mother-in-law came and opened the front door – I threw my hat in. That hat came out like a sky rocket, right across the street. That was my welcome! And I thought, oh. But I wangled, I used my charm, and Edie – she had to write and tell the sailor that it was off – took his ring off. And we had that ten days together and we knew we wanted to get married and everything she liked I liked, and there you are.

As a single boy I loved every minute of my life at sea. I was at sea four years fishing, six and a half in the Navy – all the war – and I just loved the sea, I was happy on board boats, I knew boats, nothing ever worried me really, single boy. Then of course after I met my wife – well that was different. So I got married at the end of the war and I would have liked to come ashore then. But circumstances prevented it; I'd got to get a living, and my only qualifications were a skipper's certificate. So I had to go back fishing, and we'd only been married a few weeks when I had to go away on my first voyage for 13 weeks as a mate. Oh, it was awful! I fell out of love with the sea simply because I wanted to be with my bride, didn't I, and I wanted to set up a family life and be there but I had to go back to sea because that was my living, but I would have dearly loved to have been ashore.

Then I got a daughter, Patricia, and now she just didn't know me from Adam – in fact she resented me. What few nights I was at home with my wife, my wife gave me all the attention and my daughter, she'd been used to my wife's whole attention, hadn't she, and that was all she wanted, so she'd say 'When's Daddy going back to sea?'.

Well, one way we had of keeping in touch with home was on the ship's radio. We all had Marconi transmitting ship-to-shore radios, which was very nice, so we could all then communicate with each other and we could also communicate with the shore. Now, they brought out a home radio set because we transmitted on short wave on what they called the 'trawler band', and all the fishing vessels in the U.K. could transmit on that waveband. Range fifty, sixty miles [80–95 kilometres] perhaps. And we'd call home at a set time – that was the highlight of your family's day. We'd whistle a tune or we would say, 'Hello, hello, hello, are you about there? This is George calling; over.' We couldn't hear anything back but apparently they'd say, 'There's Daddy, there's Daddy!'. Then you would say, 'Hello me old darling, here we are... yeah no luck, no fish tonight. Shan't be in today, hope to see you tomorrow. Hope everything is all right. God bless, bye-bye. Kiss for the kids.' That was it. Mummy would say 'That's your daddy', but all my daughter could see was the black radio and that was the only connection you'd got. Then she began to associate me with the man in the box. And she'd say, 'Are you my real daddy or are you the daddy in the box?'.

Then I joined the merchant navy for three years and I swallowed the anchor after that. I was not getting home at all and I made up my mind – we were going into Yarmouth – made up my mind I was going to finish with my company. So now I finished, and I then thought to myself, 'Well that's a clever trick; you've now put yourself out of work, you've got no job', but I didn't care. I wasn't going to go back to sea any more. And I got a little job in a concrete works. Nothing startling at all, but wasn't it beautiful to be able to go home when you finished work, knock off at half past five and go home on my bike and there was my wife and my daughters knowing me, knowing I was going to be there again the next day. And that continued for a short period... and then my luck turned, didn't it, and I got employed by Birds Eye Frozen Foods. Initially I wouldn't give up the sea for anything. As a single boy I would have gone back to sea if I'd known it was going to kill me. I was hooked. But once I went to Birds Eye I was a confirmed landlubber and I loved it. And my life has been all roses ever since.

GEORGE FIELD

George remembers his poor childhood in Wandsworth, London, where he was born in 1914, with a mixture of pain and pride. His father was a heavy drinker who took little notice of his children. To help the family George worked at various jobs from the age of seven, until finally he was able to escape to sea when he was 21. It was this experience – of travelling the world and seeing places he had only dreamed of – that was to change George's life forever. On the outbreak of war in 1939 George joined the merchant navy and, later, the Royal Navy. After he was demobbed he went into the building trade and now lives quietly with his wife Dodo in a flat in Paignton, south Devon. They have two sons and five grandchildren.

When I was around twelve years of age another kid off the street where I lived was going to Southend with his family for the day. When he returned I asked him if he could tell me what the sea looked like, and all he said was 'It's just a straight line. Water. Nothing else.' And I tried to visualize what it would be like.... It wasn't until I joined the Boys' Brigade and we had an annual outing to Herne Bay on the Kent coast that I first saw the sea – and I was shattered by the vast line all the way along on the horizon. Whilst I was at camp I spent sixpence of my meagre pocket money and went on a trip along the coast on a small boat and I laid over the bow looking at the water lapping around the bow of the boat, then looking out to sea and thinking that there was other countries beyond that line. And I made up my mind that I'd make the sea my ultimate goal.

After that I used to walk from where I lived to Tower Bridge and lean over and look at the ships and I used to look at their sterns – Kobe, Japan; Seattle, USA; Copenhagen – all their names where they came from. I used to see the seamen walking about the deck and their loading and unloading. And I used to

George Field with his wife and children in the early 1950s. It was this photograph which made George finally decide to leave the sea for ever.

think how lucky they were to be on those ships heading down the river and going right across an ocean to the other side of the world. I thought travel in those days was the ultimate.

I got my first ship when I was 21. It was difficult, there were so many unemployed seamen. I thought she would be beautiful, with shining brass and a cabin for every seaman, but when I saw this ship – she was called *Emerald Wings* – she was a rust bucket. It should have gone to the breaker's yard years before. When I walked into the fo'c'sle the stench and the smell were so bad I walked straight out and I began sleeping on the deck. The toilets were like sentry boxes and they were filled up with old excreta... you couldn't use the toilet at all to begin with because it was solid. But it didn't bother me that much, it was so great to be at sea.

I used to feel great as you'd hear the first officer shout 'Let go for'ard, let go aft, slow ahead', and the ship would pull away from the quayside – and it used to give me a lift. I used to think, it's away from the land, you're on the sea, and when the land disappeared you could walk around the ship and see nothing but the horizon. It meant more to me than anything else. I felt that I was achieving what I set out to do as a child. The further I went the better I felt, going from one country to another. As you came up on, say, Madagascar you could smell the nutmeg in the air long before you saw the island. I loved exploring places. You left the main port and you'd see the normal people that lived in these places. And we used to enjoy the food that they used to eat and their way of life, and all this meant a lot to me. I really thought travelling around the world I really thought I was somebody. I was doing something no other kid would even dream of doing where I was born. On the move all the time.

I came home very seldom once I started travelling around the world, but when I did I used to walk up and down in the small room where we lived. Used to drive my mother mad because on ship when you're not on watch you walk around the ship regularly for exercise and I used to walk up and down the room and drove my mother crazy. She used to tell me 'Sit down, for God's sake'.

I met Dodo on leave, but I wasn't greatly interested I'll be honest. Anyway, when I went back to my ship I asked her if she'd write because I never used to get any mail from anybody except my mother, and she did. From then it sort of went on and I kept seeing her on leave. And from then on it sort of grew and grew until I realized that when I did go back off leave I missed her badly. Then my doubts took over again and I got frightened of being tied down if we got married. And it wasn't until I went out in the Mediterranean – it was wartime – that I began to think of her in terms of really settling down. I saw so many deaths out there and misery that I thought, well, there's got to be a better life than this, and I made up my mind. As we got near Tunis I sent her a cable to ask if she would get married and, if she agreed, would she arrange everything.

Having married my wife I was committed to that life and I knew there were certain obligations I'd have to live up to. I knew that I'd have to give up the sea when the war was over, which I did do. But I had no idea how difficult it would be to give up the sea. We sat on this part bench in Richmond Park – we'd gone out for a walk in the afternoon. I wanted to be with my wife on my own, I didn't want my mother-in-law there. Our troubles were being aired and she was giving her advice, but I was losing control and it was jarring and jarring on me all the time until I just stood up and pulled this pistol I had from the war I kept on me. I don't know what I said, but I was going to fire at her and my wife. And I was horrified when I calmed down and I thought of my child in the pram there – he'd have finished up an orphan.

When I decided to leave I didn't even tell my wife I was leaving; I just went to Southampton and I was hoping to get a ship out and I'd be back to normal. Well, I arrived at this bed-and-breakfast place. I just took my bag up to the room and I just had a few things in it. I had a double-fold photograph and I put that on the dressing table. In the evening I went out and got fish and chips and I took it back there and I sat on the bed eating fish and chips and I picked the photograph up and there were my two kids looking at me, my wife was looking at me, and I felt rotten. I felt obviously I wasn't doing the right thing and I knew that if I did break away it could break us up completely. And then I thought she can marry someone else and they can bring my two children up. So I decided I wouldn't have that and I came back, and that was it. I just forgot the whole thing and got down to building up a business. But it was still very hard to settle down after that.

CAPTAIN MERVYN WINGFIELD

Mervyn was 13 when he arrived at Dartmouth Royal Naval College in 1924. It heralded the start of a career at sea that was to span nearly fifty years and which he remembers with great clarity and dry humour. Sitting in his comfortable Surrey home surrounded by seafaring memorabilia, Mervyn looks like the archetypal naval officer from a lost age of Empire. He married Sheila in 1936 and they had a daughter and two sons. After retiring in 1972 Mervyn devoted much of his time to sailing, a hobby that he still enjoys.

In 1920 the battleships *Queen Elizabeth* and *Warspite* paid a visit – a sort of victory cruise after the end of the first war – and they called in at Dublin Bay and there was a children's party given on board the *Queen Elizabeth* and we had a most marvellous day, then sat down to a most delicious tea and the tea was so good in the wardroom that there and then I decided the Navy was for me.

So I eventually went to Dartmouth, and we were very proud to be joining the Royal Navy because in those days we really did rule the waves, we were proud of the uniform and we were very pleased to be there. On the face of Dartmouth College there's the quotation: 'It is on the Navy under the good providence of God that the wealth, safety and prosperity of this nation do chiefly depend'. So we knew where we stood. We had a rather slanted form of history because it was all naval history and we were taught that the British had never ever lost a battle at sea – I only realized that we had lost to the French and the Americans much later. Every school day started with a plunge in a small bath full of two or three feet of cold water and we all had to go through this as quickly as

Mervyn Wingfield (left, sitting) and his wife Sheila (second left) at one of the many parties thrown for officers in Hong Kong. Social occasions like these were part and parcel of being in the upper ranks of the Royal Navy during the inter-war years.

possible 'cos it was jolly cold. This was supposed to reduce our sexual urges, I'm told, but it wasn't very successful, I don't think.

We were, as cadets at Dartmouth, all of the type who would normally have been at public schools. We'd all been at prep schools – except one boy. He hadn't... there was a rumour that he'd been in a council school, so we didn't pay much attention to him, but everybody else came from, oh, the upper, the middle or upper-middle classes. A tremendous number of Service parents, fathers, had been in the Services. My family had all been in the Army, but my mother said she didn't want me to go in the Army because the Army, she said, in peacetime is an idle and dissolute life. When I said I'd like to go in the Navy she said 'Well, that's better, they're more like a police force'.

When we finished at Dartmouth we went to sea as cadets and we became midshipmen, and I was appointed to a coal-burning battleship, HMS *Benbow*. It was raining and we had our Burberries on with our collars turned up. We were met by the officer who was known as the 'snotties nurse' – the officer in charge of midshipmen – and he said we were a scruffy-looking lot. 'Sub-lieutenant,' he said, 'take 'em down to the bathroom and give 'em four cuts each; we want them to look like young officers, not like hooligans.' So we were taken down to the bathroom and given four cuts of the cane. We thought 'This is quite a ship isn't it, terrific'. Because we were used to this at Dartmouth – strict discipline and immaculate tidiness, they were all important, it was all part of the fun of being in the Navy.

I trained to be a submariner and I was very pleased to be appointed to the Far East, to a submarine called *Odin*, which I joined in 1934. Now the China Fleet was seen as the best fleet – the most enjoyable, we thought, because you travelled all over the Far East. There isn't a creek or bay in the Far East I haven't visited. We did some training – torpedo firing, gunnery, manoeuvres, landing parties. We were cruising around some of the most interesting and enjoyable places in the world and we took full advantage of all they had to offer. I played a lot of golf, we did expeditions and a lot of sailing; it was a very pleasant life... often referred to as 'subsidized yachting'.

We all had Chinese boys; they were very useful and they were very pleased to get the small amount of money we paid them. I got mine from the caddy master for ten dollars – and he was mine. He came on board the submarine and he was delighted, he worked in the wardroom, waited at table, made up the bunks and looked after me. Very nice... he was more like a pet than a friend. Eventually he was signed on in the Royal Navy as a locally enlisted steward and unfortunately he went down in the *Odin* when she was sunk in the war.

I was married in July 1936 and I was very pleased my wife was able to come out and live with me. We lived ashore in a flat in Hong Kong, and as I spent a lot of time in port it was just like going to the office ... I came ashore at tea time back to my wife. Then there was a very intense social life in the evenings – dinner parties and cocktail parties with the other officers and their wives; all very smartly dressed, and it was a very happy time. And when we cruised around to Singapore, Saigon, the Philippines, places like that, the wives would follow us in coastal steamers and stay in hotels there. I always used to say I had a wife in every port – but it was always the same one!

JOHN COCKLE

There are few people living in Truro today who have not heard of John Cockle. He was born there in 1912, the son of a sailor from Ghana and an English mother. He was the eldest of five sons. He has always been fiercely proud of his heritage and the seafaring tradition of his forefathers, which eventually led him to go to sea on sailing schooners at the age of 16. A natural storyteller and mimic, John tells his tales with a youthful twinkle in his eye. He was happily married – though, by his own admission, not always faithful – to Edith for over 50 years. They had three sons. After he left the sea in 1970 John had various jobs and, in later years, was also very successful as a city councillor. He now lives alone in a terraced house overlooking his beloved Truro.

John Cockle with his wife Edith in the mid 1930s. John found it impossible to remain faithful as he travelled the world in search of adventure.

In those days ships were slow, coal-burning; some of them were motor ships, but they none of them were fast, and of course by the time a man got down to the River Plate ready to discharge the cargo he was ready to enjoy himself. The reputation that Buenos Aires had was for all manner of fun and we were happy to go down and look for a bit of titillation. There was women everywhere and those women were good! They knew how to handle themselves and they knew how to handle men. They'd invariably prevail on you to buy them a drink. We all buy them drinks…some is green and some is blue, and when you put your tongue in it, well, all it is was was coloured water, but of course the girls got commission on that you see. They would wheedle every last penny out of our pockets and we'd get drunk – and we'd enjoy getting drunk because there was some lovely bit of stuff would stroke our head and then invite us into their beds.

But having enjoyed ourselves we'd get outside and find the Buenos Aires police there – some mounted, some in 'hurry-up' wagons – complete with carbines and big knives. Now I was unfortunate enough on one of these occasions to get a bash across the shoulders, either with the butt of a rifle or a sword blade, and I went on the ground. I was pushed into the paddy wagon. There were eight or ten others besides me and they took us away to the police station. You'd be amazed who was there. Officers, gentlemen, stewards, firemen, all sorts and conditions of people, all people connected with the ships. And in the morning we were all given brooms and shovels and taken to the city's stables and we had to sweep them out and pick up all the horse manure.

My wife was a local girl in the little fishing village of Mevagissey. When I was there one night in March 1933 I saw those legs moving to and fro and I says to my mate, 'If she's all over like her legs, she's all right', and, lo and behold, she was a wonderful woman. I never ever regretted marrying that woman. We got married very quickly one time I came back and for the honeymoon I took her out on our ship, a schooner. It was wintertime, January, and believe me it was ice and snow and fog. And we set sail round the Lizard and up to the Clyde – well, what a honeymoon trip for a girl! We ate scouse – the seaman's meal, scraps of meat and vegetable – but she survived it and we came back to Truro and, well, we lived happily ever after that.

Many people think of seafarers as having a wife in every port. 'Tisn't true – they only have wives in some ports. Being the sort of person I am one woman was no good to me. I didn't set out to hurt her. I went with other women because they were part and parcel of my life. During the war my ship was trading to London for a brief time and a woman I knew, Kathleen, came into the pub. I looked at her and she looked at me and we said, well this is it. Had a couple of drinks, then we returned to her sister's house and that night we went to bed, and I went to bed with her on many nights after. Of course, when Kathleen told me she was pregnant I said, what am I going to do? So I went and told my wife. My wife was highly indignant. There were one or two sharp words and then she shut up. She did not continue to reproach me, she did not make a mountain out of a molehill. She was a good woman, a real seafarer's wife, she understood. Kathleen put the little girl in an orphanage. She got in touch with me much later – in fact I saw her quite recently.

I loved being married and at home, but after I'd been at home a while I'd get a complaint called 'itchy feet'. I used to think to myself, let's see if there's anything in Falmouth or walk along the quays in Truro. I wanted to get away, get away from the domestic environment. Not that I didn't love my wife, not that I didn't love my kids, but I liked my ship. I liked my sea, I liked the big open spaces, like most other sailors. Some would say we were selfish individuals, but I don't think so. There are always going to be people like us who enjoy wandering around… born wanderers.

ADRIAN SELIGMAN

Adrian shocked his family when he dropped out of Cambridge University in 1929 to run away to sea – he became a messroom steward on a small steamer trading to Spain. Since then he has defied convention and even now, at the age of 86, he is still searching for new challenges. Adrian was born into a middle-class

academic family in Surrey in 1909 and yearned for adventure from an early age. But it was the romance of sailing ships which lured him most of all and inspired his round-the-world voyage on the *Cap Pilar* for two years from 1936. He was married in that year and had four children, then divorced and married Rosemary in 1949, with whom he has two sons. Adrian continues to write after the success of his books *The Voyage of the Cap Pilar* and *The Slope of the Wind*.

My grandfather died aged ninety-three and left all his grandchildren £3500 – which was an enormous sum of money in those days, and I wondered what on earth I would do. I thought I must perhaps set myself up in the City somewhere, but it seemed a terribly dull sort of life to me. And suddenly it occurred to me that with £3500 I could probably buy a small ship and go voyaging around the world. I eventually bought an old Grand Banks barquentine, and to get the crew I decided to put an advertisement in the personal column of *The Times*. It said: 'Voyage to the South Seas in small schooner. Young men needed for crew, each to contribute £100 towards cost of the voyage.' Well, I got four hundred applications, and out of those 400 we chose seventeen. I can't remember on what grounds we chose them, but one of

Above: **Adrian Seligman on board *Cap Pilar*, the sailing ship he took around the world in 1936.**

Left: **The three-masted schooner *Cap Pilar* anchored off one of the South Seas islands in 1937.**

them was a doctor, one of them was a builder's labourer, another was a solicitor, another a scientist... but they were all dead keen to go to sea and sail to see the South Sea Islands. None of them had been to sea before and two of them hadn't even seen the sea, but we made out.

I took my wife Jane with us too. We had just got married and this was to be our honeymoon voyage. I remember after we'd stored the ship with provisions being towed down the River Thames and Jane's mother was standing on the jetty watching us go. She must have felt very worried to see her 20-year-old daughter being taken to sea by a sort of piratical 26-year-old young man who'd never been a skipper in his life, but there we were, we believed in each other, and that's how it all started.

The *Cap Pilar* had no engine, and we had no radio or wireless set of any kind on board. We were out, I think, to discover the world and to see whether a crowd of young people could live happily together away from any sort of civilization or the modern world, but above all we were out to discover ourselves.

The first night was a pretty rough night for us. There was high sea already and the wind was freshening. Most of the lads succumbed to seasickness, until there were only three or four of us left on the deck of the ship. One lad came up from below, I remember, to take the wheel so that the rest of us could work on the sails. That was young Peter Roache, the youngest in the ship, and he had a bucket lashed to his belt into which he was sick from time to time while he was steering.

In the old days of sailing ships they'd shanghai crews off the streets and byways – men who'd never been to sea before – and they learned very quickly Within a day or two any healthy young man will know more or less what he has to do on a sailing ship, and so it was with us. But the first time you go aloft it is a bit of an adventure, certainly. You have to get used to the roll and the rhythm of the ship – your body reacts to the life in the ship and you follow that rhythm.

It's easier than being aloft when the ship is in dry dock because then your body has no rhythm to follow. And when you're furling a sail you're all spread out along the yard and you've got to keep together, no one must let go, because the others might be dragged down on to the deck if that happened. And when there's a wind in the sail you've got to hang on for dear life, all of you together. Togetherness, fellowship, comradeship with your fellow shipmates, this is what a sailing ship breeds best of all.

It wasn't until we were well south of the Equator that we saw and caught our first shark. The cook had a sharp hook attached to a stout line and a shark had taken the bait. We all managed to haul the shark aboard; then the shark was flailing around the deck – crashing into this, crashing into that, snapping at anything he could see … eventually it was killed with a twelve-inch carving knife. And we cut the fins off for soup, to make shark-fin soup, and the tail had to be nailed to the mast for luck. That was our first shark.

We went across thousands of miles of sea to the South Sea Islands, which none of us had ever seen before. There was a little village that hadn't been visited for a long time by any schooner, and they were so pleased to see us. They came out in their canoes and surrounded the ship and took us ashore. And wherever we went they followed us, simply longing to meet our every wish or even invent our wishes sometimes. We had two weeks in the islands. They slaughtered a pig in our honour, which was a tremendous sacrifice for them as they had very little food on the island except for fish, and they put garlands on our heads. By then we had a three-month daughter, Jessica, which Jane had during the trip; she was brought forward, covered in flowers and named Atolnowa, which means 'cloud within the rainbow', and she became queen of the island for a day. When we left they followed us in their canoes – great flotillas of canoes sailing alongside us – then it was goodbye to the South Sea Islands.

When we arrived back we'd been two whole years almost to the day away from Britain. We'd been round the world, we'd seen country after country that none of us had ever seen before. We'd seen all sorts of weather, and all states of sea – storms, calms – and skies. And the crew were now, most of them, quite experienced sailors. It was a great adventure and for all of us our lives had been enriched by that voyage round the world.

2

Sea Harvest

Of all those who work on ships it is the fisherman who has the closest and most personal relationship with the sea itself. The merchant seaman travels from one port to another, the Royal Navy rehearses or fights battles on the waves, but the fisherman is in touch with the natural world of the ocean, grappling with nets to extract the fish from the sea. Fishermen, in the past, have often been seen as almost a race apart – the last true hunters, whose occupation has remained essentially unchanged since time immemorial. With their sou'westers, oilskins and sea boots, often speckled with silvery fish scales and slime, there was certainly no mistaking their calling. What marked them out most of all from other men was the extraordinary harshness and danger of their work. The fisherman knew that every time he set sail and left the safety of the harbour he was risking his life – his was by far the most hazardous job in Britain.

Yet, despite the risks shared by all fishermen, there were many regional differences in the working lives and the culture of the different fishing communities around the British coast. Even the accident and death rates varied enormously according to where and what you fished. In the small fishing ports of Devon and Cornwall – where fishermen rarely ventured far from the shore – it was very low, whereas in Hull, the centre for deep-sea Arctic trawling, it was almost ten times as high.

During the first decades of the century Britain had one of the most prosperous fishing industries in the world. In the 1920s it still boasted a fishing fleet of

around 20,000 vessels and employed more than 100,000 people. Much of the fish was sold at home, where cod, herring, pilchards, haddock and 'fish and chips' were well established in the British diet. But the export of fish was also big business – on the eve of the First World War more than three-quarters of the massive herring catch was sold abroad.

There were fundamentally two different kinds of fishing community in Britain at the beginning of the century. First there were the hundreds of coastal villages and small ports like St Ives in Cornwall, famous for mackerel and pilchards, and Buckie in northeast Scotland, where herring was the most important catch. Here, there was a tradition of small-scale fishing that sometimes went back for centuries, passed down through the generations. Many of the boats were owned or worked by families or small groups of friends and families. Tommy Morrissey, whose account appears later in this chapter, remembers being brought up to take his place in his father's fishing business in Padstow, north Cornwall, before the last war.

The women – wives, mothers, sisters, daughters – played an important role in line fishing families, gathering limpets and mussels for bait, baiting the hundreds of hooks on each long line, mending the nets and hawking fresh fish carried on the back in heavy baskets. It was almost impossible for a man to fish for a living if he didn't have a woman at home helping him. The wives knew they would be judged by their husbands – and by the community – on their ability to help with the fishing. Peggy Robinson married fisherman Jack in Newbiggin, Northumberland, in 1944.

'I did feel worried when Jack asked me to marry him because I hadn't baited lines before. But I persevered, there was such a lot of baiting to do. Then one day, a good while after we'd been married, my father-in-law came in the front door. He said to Jack "Who's baited the line?". Jack says "Peggy's baited it", so my father-in-law said, "Well Jack, you could fish with anyone on a line like that because it's well baited". And that meant such a lot to me.'

In this traditional fishing economy the boats typically stayed fairly close to the shore. They fished with lines or drift nets, trips lasted only a day or two and the proceeds of the catch were shared fairly equally among the men. For many fishing families it was a struggle to make ends meet – the earnings of the average inshore fisherman were similar to that of the lowly paid agricultural labourer – and the fish they caught formed an essential part of the family's diet. A bad

Two Cornish fishermen in 1906. With their sou'westers, oilskins and seaboots, fishermen had always been seen as a race apart.

season or a few unsuccessful fishing trips could bring real hardship and poverty to a family. Nevertheless, this spartan way of life bred a distinct culture in which there was great pride and independence, a spirit of thrift, self-reliance and sobriety – and a strict moral code which, in parts of Cornwall and Scotland, was wrapped up in fervent Evangelicalism.

Netting the dense herring shoals which, every year, used to follow a time-honoured path encircling the British coast formed the most important part of this fishing economy. The herring industry had grown hugely in size from the nineteenth century onwards with the invention of salted herrings, kippers (split smoked herring) and whole smoked bloaters. The season opened around May in the Western Isles as the first herring appeared, after which they emerged in the south, ending up off the East Anglian coast between October and December. Fleets of sail and steam drifters pursued them – many following them down from Scotland – and huge catches of herring were netted, which were then dispatched the length and breadth of Britain on the new railway network. Herring became a popular food in the working-class diet and, on the back of this boom, Buckie in the north and Great Yarmouth and Lowestoft in the south became the undisputed centres of the herring trade. Herring fisherman George Rushmer from Lowestoft recalls the joy of a big catch.

'Every net you hauled in there was a new expectancy. You'd perhaps got ninety nets out there… you'd haul them in and some might be empty, then one might be absolutely full of herring. Well, what a lovely sight! A net full of silver herrings all alive and kicking. And on a nice moonlit night it was quite exhilarating really – you would see hundreds of boats all around you all with their deck lights on all doing the same as you.'

Women played a vital role in all this, mending drift nets, gutting and kippering. Most celebrated of all were the many thousands of Scottish 'herring girls' – like Mary Coull from Peterhead – who travelled south on trains every year, following the seasonal movements of the herring boats, gutting and packing the fish in barrels in English ports like Great Yarmouth and Lowestoft. Standing on stones on the quayside, exposed to the elements, the herring girls worked at extraordinary speed – they reckoned to gut 20,000 herring in a long day – and were paid piece rate. Despite the immensely hard work and the fact that their hands were often swollen and ulcerated from the salt that entered into cuts, the young women had a reputation for their cheerfulness, singing hymns while they worked, dancing in the evenings and taking advantage of freedom from home to meet potential husbands – usually Scottish fishermen who were also following the herring.

Landing the catch at St Ives, Cornwall in the 1900s. Many of the boats were owned by fishing families – every member was expected to help out.

The heyday of the herring boom was around the turn of the century, but from the 1920s it went into decline. Herring was a cheap winter food that, in an age of increasing consumer choice, was becoming less attractive. The huge East European market for herring collapsed after the Russian Revolution. And stocks of herring were plundered so heavily that the size of catches declined – by the late 1950s the North Sea herring was near extinction. The communities which suffered the most from this were the Scottish coastal villages and ports that were so dependent on the herring. Between the wars the numbers of Scottish fishermen were halved, falling to 17,000. And in the once thriving herring ports, like Lowestoft, whole boatloads of fish were dumped back into the sea. George Rushmer recalls: 'Dumping those herrings that we'd caught was a very depressing feeling. The whole crew were despondent, weren't they. You'd work hard to get 'em, then there was no market, so after you came into port you'd have to go back and chuck 'em back into the sea. Heartbreaking.'

In stark contrast to the decline of these traditional fishing communities in the first decades of the century was the prosperity of the big deep-sea trawler ports. Deep-sea trawling began in the nineteenth century with the development of trawl nets and steam-driven trawlers designed to catch huge quantities of cod. The richest fishing grounds were in the North Sea, and the trawler ports – the biggest of which were Grimsby, Hull, Aberdeen and, on the west coast, Fleetwood in Lancashire – enjoyed an extraordinary period of expansion, backed by the railway companies. By 1914 Grimsby was the premier fishing port in Britain, with over 500 steam trawlers and 6000 men. It was sending out thirteen fish trains every day, helping to supply 20,000 fish and chip shops in the rapidly expanding towns and cities of England and Wales. There was little place for small family-owned boats in the new fishing industry. In the trawler ports practically all the boats were company-owned as the early steam trawlers cost about a hundred times as much to build and equip as a secondhand inshore boat. They consumed huge quantities of coal to take them long distances and ice to freeze the fish – and far more crew members were needed to operate them.

The trawlerman became the new industrial worker of the sea. In almost every respect his life on the deep-sea trawlers was far worse than that experienced by the traditional inshore fisherman. The trawlers went further out to sea, usually northwards into colder and rougher conditions. And they went away for much longer periods – two to six weeks rather than one or two days. This exacerbated the terrible, cramped accommodation (shelves to sleep on, no ventilation, no toilets) for which most fishing vessels were notorious.

The crews worked very long hours. A 100-hour week was common – with occasionally as much as 72 hours without a break gutting the fish on deck to prevent decay. This, again, was very different to the inshore boats and herring drifters, which made frequent visits into port and where the preparation of the fish was done by the women ashore. Incessant gutting, sometimes in Arctic conditions, inflicted enormous damage on the trawlerman's hands, which were marked by cuts and sea boils and frequently became bent and mutilated.

A herring fisherman in Lowestoft in the 1940s. Hundreds of steam drifters set off from ports all around Britain to follow the massive shoals of herring for eight months of the year.

Above: **The crew of a Fleetwood deep-sea trawler shooting the nets. Accidents were common on these boats – to be a trawlerman was the single most dangerous occupation in Britain.**

Right: **Scots Herring girls splitting and gutting the fish in Great Yarmouth in 1948. East Anglian fishing communities would be transformed every season as thousands of the 'lassies' arrived by train from Scotland.**

To cope with the harshness and brutality of the work many turned to drink. While drinking at sea was almost unheard of among inshore crews, it was common practice for deep-sea trawlermen and was seen as a serious social problem – 'the curse of the North Sea' – in late Victorian and Edwardian times. The Mission to Deep Sea Fishermen had mission ships that sailed out with the fleets of trawlers providing medical care, cheap cigarettes and, in the hope of saving lost souls, temperance lectures and rousing chapel services.

Deep-sea trawling was by far the most dangerous kind of fishing. A series of official investigations discovered an extraordinarily high accident rate. Trawler-

men spent much time on an open deck in a jolting sea with only a low rail to protect them and they worked with unguarded winches and dangerous machinery. Fractures, injured backs and severed fingers were all commonplace. Exhaustion through overwork made accidents even more frequent and those who suffered injury often had to wait several days until the boat came into port before they received proper medical attention.

Most shocking of all was the death rate. From 1884, when records of deaths at sea were first kept, more than 2000 men and boys were lost in ten years. Hundreds of trawlermen continued to die every year in the winter storms in the grey wilderness of the North Sea. The most dangerous voyages were those made into the Arctic, where the weather conditions were worst – by the 1930s many were trawling further north as supplies of cod became depleted.

Below: **The busy quayside at Great Yarmouth in the middle of the herring fishing season in 1934.**

Overleaf: **An illustration of the 1930s shows the use of small rowing boats in box fleets on the high seas. They would be used to carry boxes of fish to a fast ship – a dangerous procedure which sometimes had fatal consequences.**

Around half went down with their ships, a quarter were washed overboard and, in the first decades of the century, about a quarter were drowned in the hazardous business of 'trunking' fish. Trunking involved the men in the trawling fleets getting into small rowing boats while on the high seas to take trunks of the fish they had caught and load them into the fast boat that would return to port every day with the fresh catch. It was a dangerous, terrifying job and sometimes not even the stoutest small boat or the most skilful seamanship was a match for the huge waves that pounded them against the side of the ship as they bobbed up and down. Harry Downs from Hull recalls dicing with death as he worked on these small boats in the North Sea in the 1930s.

These dangers inspired the men and women of Britain's fishing communities to become some of the most superstitious in Britain. The superstitions were held by the women, as a kind of magical control and protection against the constant threat of death to husbands, sons and fathers. In Hessle Road in Hull – the base for Arctic fishing from the 1920s onwards – it was generally believed that a woman should not wash her man's clothes on the day he sailed or he would be washed overboard; she should never wave him goodbye or a wave would sweep him from the deck; and women were strictly taboo on the fish dock when the trawlers were due to set sail for the Arctic.

To be a trawlerman was such an unattractive job that owners turned to orphanages, reformatories and workhouses to bind pauper boys as apprentices on the fishing boats. Around the turn of the century about a quarter of trawler crews were recruited in this way. The young apprentices on the Hull and Grimsby trawlers were often severely beaten for the smallest mistake or misconduct, and many absconded despite the fact that they could be imprisoned for doing so. The suicide rate amongst apprentices was very high – some jumped overboard rather than face a life of cruelty and abuse.

The brutality of the work encouraged violence not only on the boats but at home. Domestic violence – often under the influence of drink – was rife among trawlermen and their families and was well documented in ports like Grimsby and Hull. This was in contrast to the inshore fishermen, many of whom were unusually considerate to wives and children. Corporal punishment of children, for example, was rare in most small fishing communities, especially in the Shetland Islands. Although some trawlermen were devoted husbands and fathers who treasured their brief spells at home, steam fishing was in general extremely destructive of family life.

Despite the human cost, deep-sea trawling was one of the most profitable areas of fishing in the inter-war years. The small inshore fisherman could not

ROYAL
PREACH THE WORD
LO 51

compete with the mass distribution of cheap cod and many were forced on to the dole queue or into the towns to search for jobs, their ageing boats laid up to rot. The worst decay of the old fishing industry was in the southwest. The only chance of survival for many was to combine seasonal fishing with work that exploited the booming holiday trade – such as providing trips round the bay or crewing on yachts.

Some inshore fishermen – especially on the northeast coast of Scotland and in the Shetland Islands – created a new independence and prosperity by buying small motor fishing boats, which were cheap to run, and specialized in white fish, pilchards or mackerel, caught in seine nets. By 1919 there were twice as many motor boats registered in Scotland as there were steam drifters. The spread of small-boat ownership was given a further boost when many took advantage of government grants after the Second World War. The Shetland Islands, Peterhead and Buckie in northeast Scotland became the centre of the new skipper–owner fishing industry. By 1950 85 per cent of Shetland boats were owned by the men who worked them.

Unexpectedly, it was these thriving communities of small fishermen who were to provide the long-term future of the fishing industry in Britain. From the 1950s onwards the trawler economy was undermined by 'cod wars' and the introduction of territorial fishing limits – first by Iceland, then by the EC. By the 1980s and 1990s the British trawler fleet would be a shadow of its former self and the old ports like Fleetwood and Hull were threatened with closure. By contrast, Peterhead had become the premier fishing port in Britain.

JACK LISLE ROBINSON

The stretch of Northumberland coast on which Newbiggin lies has long been associated with the small, flat-bottomed boats known as 'cobles'. Jack was born into this tight-knit community in 1916, and it was expected that he would follow his father into the fishing. He started work at eighteen and bought his own coble in 1942. Jack had known his wife Peggy, who was also from Newbiggin, for most of his life when they were married in 1944. They had one son. Peggy would help Jack with his boat and nets whenever she could. The loving partnership they forged through fifty years of working together is still very much in evidence. Jack retired in 1984 but still helps his nephew, who is also a fisherman.

When you're born into a fishing family you live the boats and fishing – you never think about anything else. The whole family had to work baiting lines and you were brought up to help do that before you went to school. And if Father asked you to stay off school, to gather bait on the rocks, you'd gladly do that. When you went to school you didn't know how slow to walk to get there, but coming back you didn't know how fast to run to get back to the fishing boats. Fishing was in your blood and you lived for it. When you played, well, you pretended you were fishermen, you rigged fishing boats, nets, and that was your life. During weekends we spent our whole time in this little rowing boat. And we'd dig worms and bait a bit-line and lay it out in the bay to catch flatties. I remember one Saturday we caught thirty flatties. That was in 1926... I remember it as if it was a fortnight ago.

And I'd go out with my father and my uncle and my oldest brother in their coble. Every opportunity you went out with them – didn't get paid – just to help and learn. When they were pulling the crab pots in you would have to lift them in, help get them cleaned and rebaited. I remember until I was about eleven years old I was always seasick, but of course you had to persevere to conquer that. You couldn't get your schooling done quick enough, leave school and into the boats – not another thought.

When you got into the fishing boats you learnt the trade. Now, each man when he went line fishing he had two lines with seven hundred hooks on – fourteen hundred hooks needed to be baited to take out every day he went to sea. You'd shoot the line a length of about three mile [5 kilometres], the last one had to lie about an hour on the sea bed, then you started to pull them in. One man would be steering the boat, slowing and stopping, another pulling the lines in and another would be gutting the fish and grading them, putting them in different boxes – haddocks in one box, cod in another, whiting in another. When you got back you laid them out on the beach and the auctioneer sold them.

Jack and Peggy Lisle Robinson baiting lines together on the doorstep of their cottage in Newbiggin in the early 1950s.

It was a lot of work and there wasn't much money to be made. So it was important to marry a fisherman's daughter because you needed her to help in the fishing, baiting the lines, helping to pull the boats up and down. A line fisherman in a coble more or less depended on a good partner to do that, and if he didn't he'd have to go and get a job working ashore. So most people married into the fishing families in Newbiggin. The Robinsons married the Dents and the Dents married the Taylors. A lot of families were more or less related in some way. Now Peggy I married, her grandfather had been a fisherman, so she had a little bit of an idea, she knew how to open mussels. She hadn't baited lines, but she learnt and she did it. Peggy turned out to be a good baiter. She was quite proud when she saw a line that she had baited and she didn't mind who saw it.

Most boats in Newbiggin were family-owned and most fisherman, if they had any ambition at all, wanted their own boat or a share in one. It was like the answer to your dream to have a coble of your own – you felt on top of the world. I saved up. We were very thrifty, we didn't socialize a lot, didn't frequent pubs… just saved. And my first coble I bought second-hand; I called it *Pride of Dawn*. My first new one that I bought next I called *Random Harvest* because in our type of fishing you take everything at random – it is a sort of random harvest is your life. I had that coble eleven years.

Your great fear was losing your coble – and that happened to me once. We put the boat on the beach, which was normal, but it got caught up in some banks of seaweed; then some big swells came and burst into the boat… the boat was full of water. We struggled, but we were fighting a losing battle, and the sea was coming in, and it was taken nearer and nearer the promenade wall and then it got a good bashing… the condition of it was beyond repair. Losing my boat that day was a bitter blow. It just felt like your world's come to an end, you were really depressed. I was really heartbroken.

But I loved being at sea, the sense of freedom, being at sea in the morning and seeing the sun rise – oh, it was a great sight. You have the changing of the seasons. Now, crab and lobster fishing, that went on in Spring and Summer and Autumn, but you went salmon fishing as well during the summer months. You didn't do any line fishing until maybe September – that was the winter fishing. When you had a good catch you felt high in the saddle. You were self-employed, you didn't have a boss to tell you what to do, you were bound to no one. We didn't make a lot of money but we were happy. You hadn't to be jealous of the trawlermen who made a lot of money – that was a different life altogether. We cast our sails as inshore fishermen and we were proud of the fact that we were inshore fishermen and we kept our heads above water.

HARRY DOWNS

Harry, born in Hull in 1918, was one of seven children of an unemployed Customs and Excise worker. He first went to sea in 1932 as a 'deckie learner' on a trawler fishing off the Faeroe Islands. He married Connie in 1940 and they had a son and two daughters. Always very close to his family, Harry gave up the sea in 1946 because he wanted to spend more time with his children. Connie died in 1988 and Harry now likes to see his children, grandchildren and great-grandchildren as often as possible.

I went down the docks 'cos I couldn't get a job ashore because unemployment was rife at that time. And I got signed on as a deckie learner and we sailed out bound for the Faeroe Islands. Anyhow, it was bad weather all that time I was in her and I'm afraid I was so seasick I was incapable of moving even. After that trip, which I shall never forget, the skipper, he said to me, 'Look son, I'm afraid you're no good as a seaman,' he says, 'the best thing you can do is get yourself a shore job'. So I thought to myself, well, I'll just have to look for another ship because there was no chance of getting a shore job at that time.

I went down the dock again and I signed on as a deckie learner with Joe Kenyon on the *Jamaica*. The skipper, Joe Kenyon – he looked like a prison warder to me: big, square-set bloke, jowled, he had hands just like Yorkshire hams – he says, 'If you'll do it, I'll show you everything to do in your deckie learning time,' he says, 'but don't you be cheeky else you'll feel the parliament side of my fist'. Anyhow, I got to admit I was a bit cheeky like, especially when I got to learn the job, and one day he chased me round the deck and I thought you won't catch me and I was up the rattlings of the rigging. He followed. And he was quicker than me. We were half-way up and he caught me. What I didn't realize, he was an ex-sailor and could climb the rigging a damn sight quicker than me. And he just picked me up and he just dangled me fifteen feet above the deck and he says '*Now* be cheeky you little bugger, now be cheeky'. 'Sorry skipper, sorry skipper, I won't do it no more, I won't do it no more.'

But believe you me, he taught me a lot… he taught me in one watch to box the compass. And while we were sailing off he'd paste on the window little bits of poetry – any little advice for me it was always in poetry. He taught me the rules of the road: 'When upon your port is seen, A steamer's starboard light of green, There's nothing much for you to do, For green to port keeps clear of you. When all three lights you see ahead, Port your helm and show your red. When in danger and in doubt, Always call the skipper out.' These words of wisdom, all implanted in my memory.

Anyhow, we set off to the fleet and when we arrived it was like a big city of lights, just like finding a lost city on water in the middle of the North Sea. We'd fish and gut, then we'd pack the catch in boxes and the boxes were taken in small rowing boats from each trawler to the cutter and when the cutter was full she'd leave and steam down to Billingsgate and discharge the boxes of fish in London. Now the men were that expert at rowing, it didn't matter what the weather was like. Mountainous seas... they used to take them boxes of fish to the cutter. And there'd be about thirty or forty boats alongside the cutter discharging the boxes of fish, taking their turn. But what amazed me with my first trip was the deckies used to stand on the gunwales of the boat like ballet dancers and jump on and off the cutter with the boxes of fish as the waves went up and down.

I thought I would never be able to do that. Because if you timed your leap into the cutter wrong in heavy rolling seas, you'd have fallen down between the boats and it would be curtains. Well, about the third trip I did actually take over on the bow oar of the boat. It was exhilarating jumping on and off the cutter – a bit like surfing. Once I mistimed it and I went in. I was frightened and I thought 'Hell, I'll have to go down, down and swim forward to get clear of the boat', and I held my breath and swam away under the water and when I came up I was just level with the bow. They picked me up right away, but it was a moment of extreme fear.

It was very tough... when I was in the fleeters you weren't allowed to wear gloves. 'Get 'em off!' You did all the gutting with your bare hands, and we used to get cracks in the joints and they used to open up with the salt water. Only sissies wore gloves – that was instilled into you as a deckie learner.

You didn't get much time between trips, perhaps a couple of days. And sometimes we'd hide so we wouldn't have to go back straight away. The ship's husband, Robbie, he'd come round for you, and if we spotted him coming down the street me and my brother used to get under the table. We'd tell mum, 'Hey Nance,' – we called her Nance – 'tell him we're not in'. And he used to knock at the door: 'Where's them two buggers!' 'Oh, they've gone out...', but she'd be signalling on her face, looking downwards under the table, because she wanted us to earn the money. So as soon as me and Jack went out to the local he'd be waiting outside for us; he says, 'I want you to sign on', so we never refused.

Later we went fishing up to Iceland or Bear Island and the conditions were absolutely terrible. You got all the ice and the snow – in wintertime it's like hell on earth. I've had icicles out me nose, all my eyebrows frosted up, couldn't breathe the icy air. It was only movement that kept you going. A kind of must would come off the sea – that is, black frost – and it ices everything up on the ship. Occasionally you've got to knock off and start breaking the ice off the ship or she would turn over. We lost three ships that way – they just iced up and turned over.

The longest I've worked without sleep is 48 hours. That was fishing off Greenland... we was dropping. In fact we was that sarcastic we said 'Aye skipper, can you lend us some matches to keep our eyes open?'. To put 24 or 36 hours in was quite normal in them days. When you hit the fish, if it was heavy fishing you never got any sleep. You'd shoot, then tow for twenty minutes, get another bag, then shoot again, and you was gutting away to try to clear the fish that were piled up on the deck. You just wanted to flop out, it's just will power that kept you going. This is what the fishermen were like.

You'd have terrible backache, continually bending forward, hour after hour, hour after hour, and you're absolutely in pain doing it. And with the gutting your wrists were bent and they used to get locked in a certain position and when you tried to straighten them there was terrific pain. They called it 'the jummy lumps'... it was a severe rheumatic pain. The only cure was rest, but you couldn't do it, you had to keep on and on. And the continual chafing of your oilskin on the wrists and the salt water getting into the pores of the wrists used to bring you out in boils. There was a hundred discomforts you could describe. Once I broke my ankle and cracked two ribs in an accident on the deck but I had to keep working, keep gutting.

A skipper was God on a ship, the skipper was absolute God and you recognized his authority. The thing that was at the back of your mind was at the end of the trip he could finish with you. If a skipper saw you straightening your back he'd think you weren't gutting because you had to bend all the time, and if you had five or six minutes straightening your back, getting the kinks out, he'd say 'Aye, go on, get yer backs bent and get on with it'. He'd admonish you. He didn't like to see you stop when you was gutting the fish.

TOMMY MORRISSEY

Tommy was born in the picturesque fishing town of Padstow in north Cornwall in 1915. He is a popular, well-known figure on the quayside and in the boats, which have been his life. Born into a

fishing family, there was little doubt he would work at sea. His father ran a fishing and pleasure boat business in Padstow; his mother did the bookings and sold fish on the side. Tommy's working life on the boats began at the age of 14 on the day he was old enough to leave school. When it was no longer profitable to fish he ran trips round the bay and became renowned for his unrivalled knowledge of local folklore. Married with two daughters, he still lives with his wife in the quaint fisherman's cottage overlooking the harbour where they brought their children up.

Well, we mostly all of us young boys we lived on the quay… we never had much cash but we used to be swimming, rowing, racing up and down the river sailing boats. The harbour was full of sailing ships then, sailing coasters, ketches and two- and three-mast schooners. There was always something going on. Steam was slowly taking over from sailing ships and they used to bring coal 'ere to store for bunkering. It was always a busy, picturesque place then and tons of work. Everybody had plenty to do and most of the youngsters, soon as they left school they went to sea, but I didn't. I worked the family boat as soon as I left school – I had to do it really because Father, he nearly drowned on the Bar when he was eleven years old. The boat upset on the Bar and they pulled Father out but as they picked him up they stuck the boat-hook in his spine, so he never really grew from the waist down. Mind you, the top of him was like a gorilla! He started off skipper and eventually he bought the *Kingfisher* and he went fishing for a living. During the summer months he did a lot of tripping.

Padstow was a big herring port and from the middle of October until the first week in January all the western men came up here from Porthleven, Mousehole and Newlyn and there'd be, oh, sixty, seventy herring boats from those ports.

And when I left school he'd trained me right up to the hilt and I could do anything, so I started in the fishing in 1930. I worked three-handed – there were two crew men and myself and we had a share each, cleared expenses, and the boat had a share for maintenance and engine, nets and sails had a share. You see, we'd still got the sails 'cos none of the old boys would trust the engine – the 'motor' they used to call it. When I first took on I had two old boys with me, Bill Kellow and Joe Dalley, and they were good blokes you know, strong, and we'd go out and stop the engine and shoot the nets, say, half past three in the afternoon for the close of the evening. We'd swing round, sheet the mizzen on tight to keep her on the wind, stop the engine, and I used to go in and boil the kettle. They always had the sails ready and the oars in case the motor wouldn't go and I wouldn't be in there ten minutes afore they'd say 'You'd better come out here'. I'd say 'What's up?'. 'Try the engine' they'd say... they wanted to start 'un every ten minutes to see if he would go! They never had any faith in it at all.

Tommy Morrissey (left) and friend working on the fish quay in Padstow in the late 1920s.

Now the old man was the brains, he knew where the herring was. He was in bed but he told me where to go and the time to shoot the net and the time to haul the net. One night, off of Gull Island, we'd shot and about seven o'clock they said the toppers were looking deep – that's the floats that keep the net up out the water. The net was full of herring and it took us an hour to haul in and the old man watched everything from his bedroom window. There were 52 barrels of north Cornwall herrings and I went up to tell the old man, but he knew already by the boat – I mean he knew within a few pounds what was in that boat. I loved herring fishing, it was clean ... there was no sorting, no gutting or nothing, the herring came out clean as a whistle and they went right in the barrels. We only fished locally for the three or four months it was on.

The way it worked was we dealt with a buyer for the season. He was Brian Parkin; he bought everything and you'd come in – each boat had a flag on the mast, the Company flag – and when you come in their agent would come down and he would ask what you had. Then they would pick 'em up in the horse cart and take 'em up the fish market.

We had a big trawl season after the herring season. The herring used to start up at the east – Clovelly, Bideford – then move down and the fishing boats moved with 'em. You see we were only day boats really, 'cos of carrying the fuel. The best catches were moonlight nights, especially the first moon in December.

And, you see, all these things were handed down from father to son. All the old boys here, they taught their sons the trade and they wouldn't tell anyone else. If you got off, say, half past three in the afternoon, shot the nets just before the close of the evening, you could tell from the colour of the water. Sometimes we'd have a very fine wire on a weight and steam slowly ahead and if the fish was thick you'd feel the fish touch the wire. Another was, where the thickest of the fish were was where the gulls were circling, so that's where you shot the nets.

Sometimes the old boys said that when the fish was that thick together the blood used to come out of their gills. If you saw a big concentration of sea birds you'd have a big school of fish and the higher the birds the deeper the fish. That's why the old man put double ropes on the nets, you see; when the birds were low we'd shorten 'em. As for the marks of the grounds, they guarded that with their life. When you had the fish there was no point in rushing your guts out to come back 'cos everybody's fish was sold to their own buyer. 'Twasn't like the other fish, trawled fish – that was auctioned. The first boat in had first sale, that's the rules in Padstow.

Now, where there's fishermen there's superstitions. All sorts. Like they didn't like to see a parson – they called a parson a 'sky pilot' – and nuns, they'd hate to see nuns on the quay. There was four walking on the quay yesterday and they all disappeared... some of 'em still believe in it. It never worried me. But starting on a Friday – they'd never start a voyage on a Friday. Terrible! And down west they'd never go out on a Sunday.

I was with one skipper in a trawler, Jack Green, and he couldn't bear anybody aboard the boat with a white-handled knife ... he was in the dock here one day and he picked up a brand new knife and threw it overboard and he gave the bloke half a quid [50 pence] then and said 'Go and get yourself a black-handled knife'. Anybody whistle on a boat, God strewth! Whistling for a gale they reckon. The only thing that my father was superstitious about was umbrellas. When we did day tripping, if they put an umbrella up – oh, he couldn't stick that. They had to put 'un down right away.

My father and mother started off the first boat-hire business in Padstow. Mother used to do the bookings and Sir John Betjeman's father would come all dressed up in brogues and knickerbockers and me mother would laugh – they'd have a real good laugh together.

After the trawl season finished I used to pack up working for Bloomfields and on the first of May I would run the boat. I used to have lobster pots and go out early in the morning and do that; then I would take people out for fishing trips and parties. Some people would book a boat for the day and I used to take them out all round the coast and I'd tell 'em all the folklore about the little caves and where boats had got wrecked. Coppinger the pirate, he went across to

France to bring back a set of bells for the church and off Boscastle a nor'westerly gale came and the ship was lost and they say now that on a calm night, if you stand on the cliff and you hear the bells of Boscastle ringing there's going to be a severe gale of wind – and they still believe in the old legend now, up there.

In those days old Viscount Clifton of Lanhydrock used to go out with Father a lot and when Father got laid up I took it on. I had regular runs and the people treated me well. They used to come and collect me and take me up to Lanhydrock for dinner with 'em and the old cook always used to send me down a big hamper full of gear for Father and Mother.

Sometimes I had a job to fit 'em all in. It was 25 shillings [£1.25] for a day or five shillings an hour, but they never asked what the trip came to. Instead they'd give me money in an envelope – quietly, in my hand – and it was always double what I would charge 'em.

I started to make ships in a bottle when I was ill and couldn't work for two and a half years. And then I'd do them during the winter when it was rough weather and I couldn't get out. I used to make six a week, and I would take three or four aboard the boat to sell to the tourists or the people I had out.

Yes, I'd tell a few tales. We had lots of people who came and they'd love it, and on the fishing trips ask you all the questions – 'Is the tide right?' and 'Is the moon right?' – and they'd try and get on a trip every day of their holiday, they loved it so much.

MARY COULL

At the age of 94 Mary is becoming less active and her sight is failing, yet she still exudes a youthful innocence and enthusiasm. Her descriptions of her life as a herring lassie, spoken in the rich Peterhead dialect of her childhood, are genuinely beautiful. When Mary was born that northeastern corner of Scotland was as important to the fishing industry as it has since become to the massive oil companies which dominate the local economy. Mary married John Coull, a fisherman, in 1940. John died in 1994. She lives in a small, traditional granite cottage in Peterhead with her daughter, son-in-law and granddaughter.

I started the herring gutting when I was seventeen. I knew a bit about it because my father had a little boatie... the family were fisher folk. I'd baited the lines for Father, mended the nets and gutted the herring. The gutting started in Lerwick in June. We went over on the boats and at Lerwick, all along the coastline right out to the place where we worked it was herring yards. Oh it was lovely, Lerwick – beautiful, fresh air all day! And we started there at six in the morning and we worked all the daylight there was. Now in the summer there was a lot of daylight, and sometimes we'd have just three hours in bed before we were up again. I went with my two sisters and we had a little hut there. Every crew had its own dwelling. We did our own cooking there, it was a real home from home.

You held the herring in your hand, and you had a little sharp knife and you put it under the throat of the herring and you nipped it – that's all you did. Put the gut into your caulk and put your herring into its own tub. Speed was everything... you were paid for what you did, so you went as fast as you could.

But the salt used to get down between my fingers and made big holes in my hands. Well, my mother, she taught me how to cure it. She chewed oatcake and when she got it to a certain attitude she took it from her mouth and she stuffed those holes. They were all dressed up, then she put on cloths and you could work all day. And we never missed half an hour at our work.

We went to Yarmouth round about the first of October and stayed there until Christmas. It was a lovely journey to Yarmouth and the curer paid our fares of course. That was a thrill to me, getting a long run in a train. We lay and slept on the floors, but I loved it when we came to Newcastle and York... those big places with all the electric lights shining and the reflection in the rivers of all the lights. It was beautiful, and if I was asleep I told them to waken me up to see the bright lights.

Never had a bad landlady and I was 20 years in Yarmouth. My landladies were all something like my mother and did their best for us. Us sisters, we rose ourselves in the morning at five o'clock, made our own tea on the gas ring and went away to work. We came home after three hours work at nine o'clock for our breakfast and the porridge was ready on the table. Did our own toiletry, then away back to the gutting again till dinner time and we came home to our dinner at one o'clock, which was always on the table ready for us. We bought the food ourselves but they did the cooking. Then start again at two and we worked until seven. The locals used to come and watch us – we were quite an attraction but we didn't take any notice, we just carried on with our work. When we worked in the evenings it was always hymns that we sung because we knew all the words in the hymn book. We sang the Sankey hymns, especially 'I Have a Shepherd' – that was one of the favourites. We always started off, then the coopers joined in and everybody would be singing.

We got very tired and we were very glad that we had Sunday. We never touched a herring on a Sunday. The English fleet went out but the Scotch never loosed a rope, not a Scotch boat went to sea on a Sunday. It wasn't done amongst the fisher folk to misuse our Sunday because it was the Lord's Day. We kept it where it should be. We were brought up to revere Sunday, and we did. We went to the Baptist Church in Yarmouth, and at tea time our lodgings were packed because all our relations that were down for the fishing came for their supper and we'd make preparations for that. Had a father and two brothers were at the fishing and they came every Sunday night, aye.

It was when we were gutting in Yarmouth that we heard one dinner time when we were going home that there was going to be a strike. I said, 'I'll not have anything to do with it, I'm not going to strike'. So we came back and were gutting away and the strikers took bits of slates off the roofs – they had tiles, they had bricks, as ammunition – and they threw it at the people who wouldn't stop working. Well, what could you do, you just had to fall in with the crowd. We just stuck in our knives. Then my boss she says, 'Mary, you get three crews, we've got a little yard', and she described to me where this little yard was, but I said 'No, I'm not going to be the one to break the strike, because the strike is right'. Our pay was wrong... it was too low. And we were two and a half days on strike – had boats lying in the Yarmouth river, loaded with herring. Then they had to give in. We won, got tuppence a barrel more. Well, that made a big difference when you settled up.

DICK TAYLOR

Dick's background was firmly rooted in Hull's Hessle Road, an area synonymous with the heyday of the British deep-sea fishing fleet. His father worked on the trawlers and, before Dick was born in 1931, his mother earned money as a fish gutter. Dick went to sea when he was fifteen and became a skipper in 1960. He vividly remembers the turbulent three-year 'Cod War' that took place off the coast of Iceland between 1958 and 1961. He has been married

to Sheila for forty years and they have three children and five grandchildren. Now retired, he loves to watch Rugby League whenever he can and is a passionate supporter of Yorkshire County Cricket Club.

Well, the first cod wars, we all thought it was a bit of a lark! The general public didn't know much about it because it didn't seem important – they just wanted to move some limit lines from three to six miles [from 4.8 to 9.7 kilometres].

I remember I was in a ship called the *Imperialist* and we'd just stowed our gear, luckily. If we'd been trawling along doing about three and a half knots the Icelandic gunboat would have boarded us quite easily, but we spotted the gunboat and we started steaming at full speed. Well, that ship was quite fast for an old side-winder trawler, she could make 12 or 13 knots if the weather was flat calm. The ship was the biggest of the Icelandic gunboats and we saw her go and she got about six miles ahead of us and suddenly turned round towards us and we saw her launch the Z-boat, which is the Zodiac. Our skipper shouted out 'Get ready to stop these guys getting aboard'. I was bosun at the time. I said, 'Just get a few lumps of coal in yer hands, two of you grab the short hooks, two get the long tommy hooks, and if they try to get aboard we'll just push them off'. And they're shouting out, 'But what if they go in?'. I said 'That's their problem – if they go in the water they'll soon be picked up'. Anyway, their Z-boat got alongside of us and threw grappling irons, which hung on the ship's rail. The grappling iron had a rope, so we had sharp knives and we just cut the rope and the boat moved off again. They tried again, and one Icelandic sailor climbed on to the rail and there's one of our deck hands looking at him and talking to him and I dashed along. I said 'You stupid git', and I just pushed him in his chest back into the boat. There's no way they would have got on board. That was the only incident we had with the Icelandic gunboats in the first cod war.

When I first started as skipper I went mostly to Iceland and the limits were extended to 12 miles [19.3 kilometres] in July 1960. When you were fishing for plaice and quality fish, the closer you got to the land the more fish there was you see. There was more fish inside the limits. I saw a couple of older skippers 'having a dip', especially when it was dark, and I watched their bags of fish come up. So I thought, well, if they can do it I can do it, so I had a little dabble inside. And while you're fishing inside that limit you get in a buzz because you're on edge. You have the wireless operator… his head is inside the radar all the time. If you see any other ships appear you've got to make a rapid exit, haul your gear quick and get out, even if it's a friendly ship – for example, Aberdeen trawlers, Grimsby or Hull trawlers.

Well, I got a liking for it. I didn't always go to Iceland – I liked the Norwegian coast. Often there we went inside the limits, but the Norwegian gunboats gave you a warning. Well, that was fair. But not with the Icelanders – if you strayed inside that line they grabbed you. If I thought there was more fish inside the limits than was outside I would go in, but not stupidly. You had to know. We knew when the gunboats was hiding down the fjords – I had a pal, Ernie Johansson, used to be an Icelandic trawler skipper, he was the harbour pilot and he was very pro-British, and I struck up friendship with him and he gave me a lot of information. On your radar, if you've got another ship you get an interference like a series of dots, but if you get tiny spikes it means there's a gunboat hiding in the fjords. So we used to call 'em 'the spikes of death' on the radar. I did it for the crack, the excitement, plus the fact that it was up to you to catch the fish. If you didn't catch the fish, you know, you'd get no wages... with the crews' livings, the owner's business and your own living. So I never thought it was stealing from another government 'cos I thought that fish is going to swim outside the limits anyway.

When you was poaching on the northwest coast of Iceland you poached for plaice – that was a prime fish. We were well organized and we had a favourite spot where half a dozen known poachers would be. One used to go to about ten or fifteen miles to the east of where we were going to poach and we're in VHF contact all the time. We had Bunny Newton looking out to the west and another pal looking out to the east, and if everything was clear and I wasn't getting the spikes of death on the radar the gunboat wouldn't be down the fjords. My turn to go in, so he gets shot along the limit line and as soon as you've shot your gear then it's out all lights, everywhere, all portholes blocked up. Some of the boys used to say 'Hello, the Old Fox' – that was my nickname – 'the Old Fox is at it again!'. You'd be about an hour and a half inside the limits and you'd have to haul your gear inside the limits. When you'd finished you would steadily make your way back to the line so you was just outside the limit line when you hauled your gear and as soon as you were outside limits you could feel the tension relax. It must have been in me blood, poaching, but it just became a way of life for me.

3

Mutiny and Mayhem

Mutiny is an emotive word and not one normally associated with the supposedly loyal, stoic and good-humoured British seafarer in the first half of our century. This was the era when Britannia ruled the waves and there was immense pride in the discipline and strength of the Royal Navy. However, while this was the image that the Admiralty and the government were keen to promote, beneath the surface lay a mass of grievances and discontent waiting to explode into mutinous behaviour. In the merchant fleet and the trawling industry, too, defiance towards authority was deeply embedded in the culture of the lower deck. Occasionally this defiance sparked into full-blown mutiny. More often it took the form of covert rule-breaking, scams, deputations, desertions, protests, fights, sabotage, strikes and even riots. Many were determined to voice complaints and assert their interests despite the punitive weight of the naval and maritime laws they laboured under. Incidents like these were an embarrassment or a threat to the authorities and were normally played down or covered up, especially in wartime. As a result, only a few mutinies have been officially acknowledged and much of this rebellious activity has remained unrecorded. The only way to discover its real extent and to understand the true motives of the mutineers is by documenting their stories, which have remained largely hidden from history.

Most seamen worked under harsh or even tyrannical conditions of service, with fewer individual rights than almost any other occupation. When they enrolled in the Royal Navy, signed on with a shipping company or cargo boat or

Scrubbing the deck on board ship in 1942. Strict discipline and regulated daily routine was a fact of life in the Royal Navy.

became an apprentice or deck hand on a trawler, they put themselves under the absolute control of the captain of the ship. The expectation was unquestioning obedience to authority, justified by the danger of life at sea or the demands of war. To achieve the high level of discipline required it was regarded as important to crush any youthful rebellion and instil habits of obedience and subordination in boy seamen. Formal discipline was strongest in the Royal Navy, where rules and regulations harked back to the days of Nelson. From the moment they joined up boys were subjected to a very strict, 'spit-and-polish' regime in naval

Above: **Officers enjoy lunch in the wardroom. The enormous social gulf between the ratings and the upper ranks was reflected in their living conditions.**

Right: **The daily rum ration is measured out for eager ratings. Navy life fostered a strong sense of camaraderie amongst the men of the lower deck.**

training ships and establishments. Drill and daily inspections of kit and uniform formed an important part of the training, and any breach of discipline would be punished. Boy seamen could be caned or birched up to the age of 18. The maximum number of strokes was twelve and public beatings for serious offences were carried out in front of all the boys. From 1901 to 1992, 241 birchings and 8000 canings were recorded in naval training establishments. Naval discipline became slightly more relaxed from the 1930s onwards, but beatings of boys were still a common occurrence after the Second World War.

There were some training schools for young merchant seamen, modelled on the harsh Royal Navy training ships, but most boys who worked on the cargo boats went to sea without any formal instruction. The young deck hand was normally initiated into life at sea by being worked very hard and forced to do the most menial tasks. Any misbehaviour or failure to do his duty would often be punished with a clip across the ear or a punch from older crew members. Trawlermen had the reputation of being even more harsh with new recruits. Belts and sticks were commonly used on boys who stepped out of line.

DURING THE BRIEF PERIOD OF NAVAL UNREST: IN H.M.S. "HOOD."

AT INVERGORDON WHEN A PROPORTION OF THE LOWER RATINGS SERVING WITH THE ATLANTIC FLEET WERE DISCUSSING THE REDUCTIONS IN NAVAL PAY: IN THE "HOOD" ON THE DAY ON WHICH THE SHIPS SAILED FOR THEIR HOME PORTS, ALL "PASSIVE RESISTANCE" AT AN END.

Sailors gather on the deck of HMS *Hood* during the Invergordon mutiny in September 1931. The proposed 25 per cent cut in pay was enough to send 12,000 ratings out on strike.

The fact that punishment was so much a part of a young man's life at sea reveals not just the severity of the discipline but also the extent of the rebellion against it. Many boys obeyed and showed deference to authority only when they had to. When the opportunity arose they broke the rules. In the Royal Navy some of their most common offences were smoking, swearing, slacking and disrespect to authority. As the boys became fully fledged seamen defiant attitudes to authority often grew in intensity, for antagonism to officers or the skipper was a central feature of the sub-culture of the lower deck. Social class was extraordinarily important in shaping these attitudes. The vast majority of men on the lower deck were working class and they had little opportunity for promotion.

Class barriers were most pronounced in the Royal Navy. In the 1930s only three per cent of officers came from the lower deck and officer cadets were still selected primarily on the basis of accent, parentage and a privileged upper-class upbringing. Most officers in the merchant fleet came from a predominantly middle-class background. There was perhaps most chance of promotion in the trawling industry, but the skipper – even though he may have risen from deck hand – was often a hard man, fierce in his authority and widely seen as a tool of the fishing companies.

The abuse of authority by the captain or officers was a common provocation for protest and mutiny on a ship, especially in the first decades of the century when discipline was most severe. The captain or skipper enjoyed absolute power, but how this was exercised in day-to-day discipline varied considerably between different individuals and ships. In the Royal Navy the captain could punish his men without trial: they could be dismissed with disgrace, imprisoned for up to three months, placed in solitary confinement, stopped from receiving rum, forbidden to smoke, deprived of pay and allowances, given extra work or stood in the corner like naughty children. An overzealous captain – or even perhaps a petty officer, marine or NCO – could provoke trouble if he dealt too harshly with fairly minor offences like drunkenness, leave-breaking and gambling. In 1902 most of the 321 court martial hearings were for striking or using threatening language towards a superior officer, often as a result of a personal argument and threat of punishment. Excessive punishments provoked mass refusals of duty on a number of ships, for example HMS *Furious* in 1909, HMS *Zealandia* in 1914 and HMS *Fantone* in 1917. After the Great War slightly more lenient attitudes to discipline in the Royal Navy meant that this kind of mutiny became more rare. It was most likely to occur when a tyrannical captain was also incompetent and endangered the life of his crew – as is vividly remembered by Alan Lawton, who tried to murder the captain of his minesweeper in 1944.

Harsh discipline and the absence of individual rights in the Royal Navy encouraged those who broke the rules to do so secretly to avoid detection and punishment. This was especially the case with sexual misbehaviour. While there was tolerance or even admiration for the sexual misdemeanours of the heterosexual man, the Navy was keen to rid itself of its traditional association with homosexuality. The all-male setting of life in the Royal Navy had long attracted gay men to it. The absence of women gave them many opportunities for casual sex with frustrated heterosexuals who were missing their wives and girlfriends. But the illegality of homosexuality – both in society and in the armed forces – meant that gay men lived in constant fear of exposure, leading to the possibility of interrogation, blackmail, ruin by informants or loss of career. There are no reliable statistics on the numbers of men who resigned or were discharged for homosexuality – it came under the catch-all categories of 'disgraceful conduct' or 'conduct unbecoming' – but it is probable that there were several hundred each year. In fact there is very little documentary evidence on homosexuality at sea at all, and it is only through the stories of men like Terri Gardner, who joined the Royal Navy in 1940, that we can begin to glimpse the workings of this secret gay sub-culture.

One of the most abiding sources of discontent was pay. Of all those who worked at sea, probably worst off were lower-deck naval ratings. Although their low pay was in part compensated by the hope of a pension after 20 years service, the pension was small and many were ineligible as they did not complete the full term. There was a traditional ban on collective action by sailors, but since the early 1900s a mass movement among seamen had taken the form of lower-deck societies – the equivalent of working men's benefit clubs – which concerned themselves with pay and conditions of service. While in previous centuries the vast majority of sailors had been recruited from the naval ports and bases, more and more were arriving from northern towns and cities where trade union thinking and action were well established. The growing discontent manifested itself in a number of mutinies during and shortly after the First World War – for example the mutiny for increased pay on the patrol boat *Kilbride*, stationed at Milford Haven, Dyfed, Wales, in January 1919. As with most mutinies it was swiftly crushed and the mutineers were severely punished, receiving prison terms of between 70 days and two years.

The best-known modern naval mutiny was at Invergordon, Scotland, in September 1931, when the entire Atlantic fleet of 12,000 sailors mutinied over a proposed 25 per cent cut in their pay. Most were still being paid at the 1919 rates of around £1.50 per week for a married man with a child, and for some the reduction meant that their families would be burdened with unmanageable debt and face eviction. What made this harder to bear was the fact that officers, who enjoyed substantially higher salaries, were only faced with an 11 per cent decrease. Although there was recognition that the economic crisis would lead to pay cuts in the public sector, the ratings felt betrayed by the Admiralty and furious at the inequality of the sacrifice. On the morning of 15 September most of the seamen refused to set sail from Invergordon. Though technically a mutiny it

Cramped conditions on board a minesweeper in 1943. Sailors lived, ate and slept in the same confined space for months at a time.

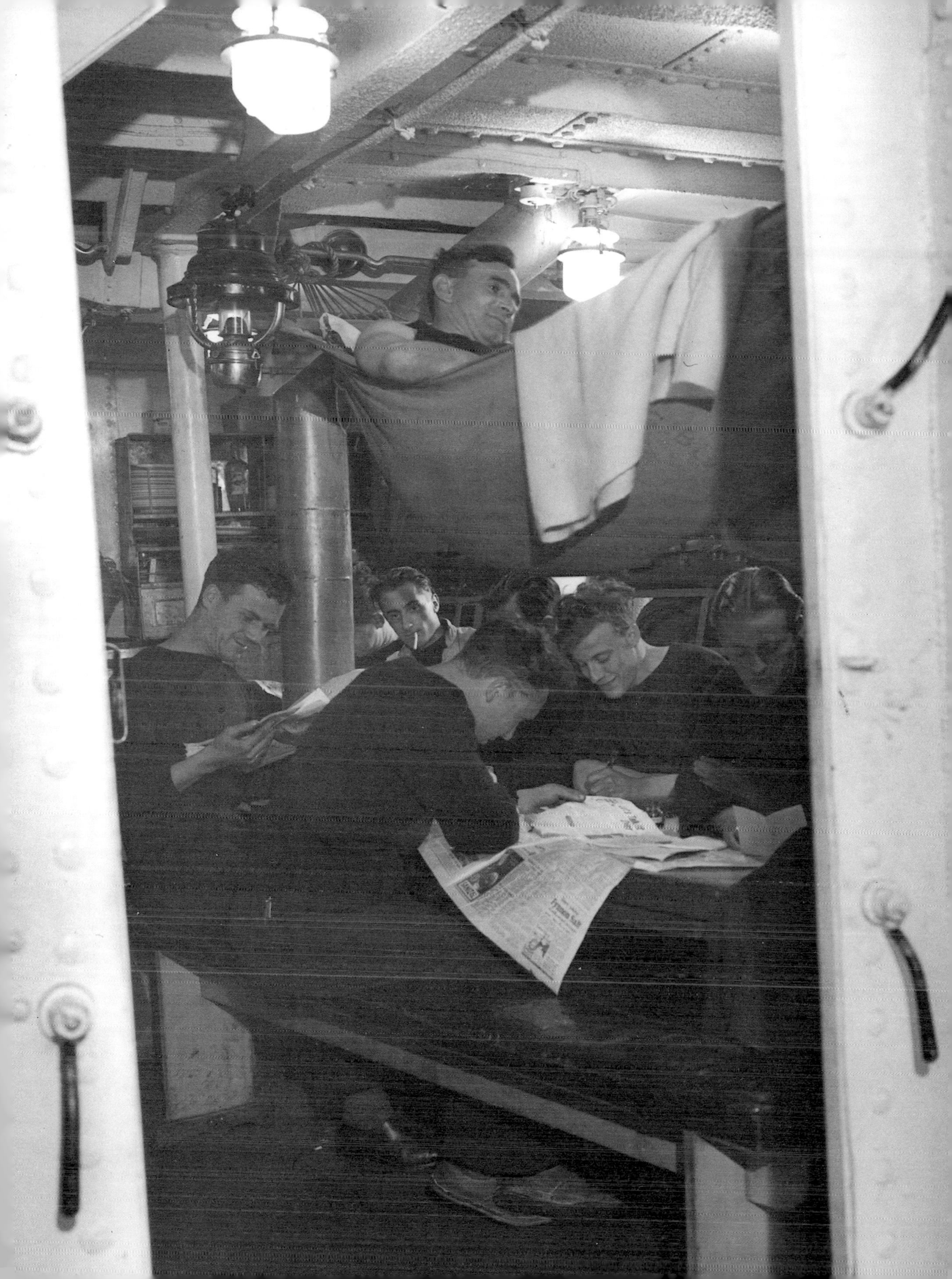

Mealtime on the lower deck during the Second World War. Bad food was a common cause for complaint and could occasionally trigger protests.

was, in effect, a strike, a remarkable act of solidarity by so many men given that it was illegal – as Tom Adams, then a rating based at Devonport, remembers.

'They called hands at six o'clock. Normally you'd do an hour's work before breakfast scrubbing the decks, and we were all in our hammocks on the mess deck and we'd all agreed we were going to stay there. I can remember plainly our Commander coming in and saying, "Come on Adams, get up, get out of the hammock", and I said, "No Sir, I'm staying here", and he went from hammock to hammock and we all said "No". We were terrified but we were exhilarated at the same time by what we'd done. When it was all over the balloon burst, everybody felt deflated – we'd achieved something though and we felt it was worthwhile.'

To defuse a dangerous and damaging situation the Government announced that it would investigate cases of hardship, and by the next day the mutiny was effectively over. To avoid further protests the pay cut was reduced to a maximum of 10 per cent for all ratings. This was the last great naval mutiny over pay.

Even among merchant seamen and trawlermen, who enjoyed the advantage of trade unions to negotiate pay and conditions, any collective action was widely seen by employers as mutinous. Their unions were notoriously weak and divided and union militants found themselves quickly blacklisted and out of work. The fact that the men worked in isolation from each other on different ships made them very difficult to organize. Strikes in ports like Aberdeen, Hull and Fleetwood during the inter-war years invariably resulted in victories for the masters. The ineffectiveness of the main union, the National Union of Seamen, led many to resort to unofficial stoppages – like those of 1947 – in protest at the reductions in pay rates. This unofficial nationwide strike action by merchant seamen provoked an extraordinarily violent response from the authorities. One of the Liverpool strike leaders, Bill Hart, was sentenced to six months' imprisonment after he tried to prevent the use of 'blackleg' labour. His graphic recollections of the strike and his own part in it appear later in the chapter.

Poor working conditions were another major grievance that could provoke mutinous behaviour. Merchant seamen on cargo boats and fishermen generally endured the worst conditions. Their basic working week was generally 64 to 84 hours, on top of which they did considerable overtime – especially trawlermen, making their working hours some of the longest in all British industry. Living and sleeping conditions were very cramped: it was common for a dozen men to be provided with double-decker bunks in one small space. With many cargo companies ratings were required to provide their own bedding, normally a palliasse stuffed with straw called a 'donkey's breakfast'. Washing and toilet facilities usually

Ratings of the Royal Indian Navy prepare to join their ship in 1942. Poor conditions and discrimination from British officers would eventually lead to unrest on a massive scale.

consisted of a bucket, to be emptied out every day. In the old steamships – still widely used up to the 1950s – the living quarters often quickly became filthy and infested with bugs or lice. Anger at the appalling conditions led to a series of illegal strikes during the last war, one of which almost held up the D-Day convoy at the London docks in April 1944. The simple demand of the seamen, quickly conceded, was for a larger piece of soap to try to keep clean.

One particular cause of resentment on the lower deck was inadequate and inferior food. Eating was segregated in all merchant and Royal Navy ships and officers would never eat with the men. More important, the food in the officers' mess was usually vastly superior to that served up on the lower deck.

This provoked a range of strategies to get revenge or a fairer share. Occasionally there would be attempts to spoil the officers' food. More often, when loading in port the ratings would redirect food bound for the officer's quarters to the lower deck. There might also be deputations to the cook or the captain over the poor quality of the food. Resentment of this sort occasionally erupted into disturbances or riots on board ship.

One of the most embarrassing mutinies in the Royal Navy during the Second World War – triggered by dreadful conditions – was that on HMS *Lothian* in September 1944. The *Lothian* was the flagship in Force X, a landing force that was dispatched from Britain halfway around the world to aid the Americans in their Pacific campaign. The mutiny is graphically recalled by Bill Glenton, one of many newly recruited 'hostilities only' ratings (see Chapter 4) who took part in it.

A more common reaction to conditions on board was to jump ship. In the early decades of the century the desertion rate in the Royal Navy was extraordinarily high, testimony to the harshness of living and working conditions. Every

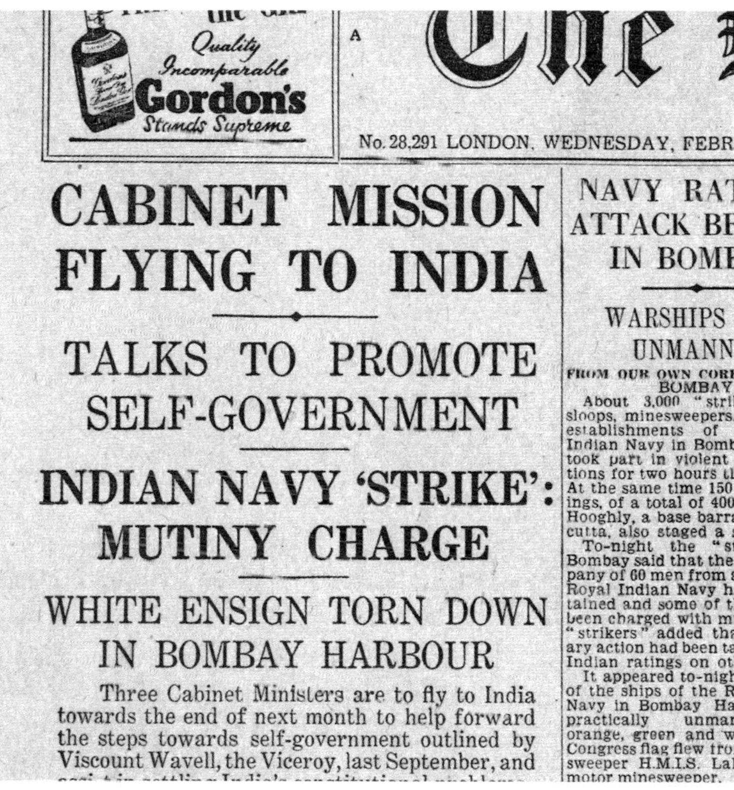

No. 28,291 LONDON, WEDNESDAY, FEBR

CABINET MISSION FLYING TO INDIA

TALKS TO PROMOTE SELF-GOVERNMENT

INDIAN NAVY 'STRIKE': MUTINY CHARGE

WHITE ENSIGN TORN DOWN IN BOMBAY HARBOUR

Three Cabinet Ministers are to fly to India towards the end of next month to help forward the steps towards self-government outlined by Viscount Wavell, the Viceroy, last September, and

NAVY RAT
ATTACK BR
IN BOMB

WARSHIPS
UNMANN

FROM OUR OWN CORR
BOMBAY,

About 3,000 "stri
sloops, minesweepers,
establishments of
Indian Navy in Bomb
took part in violent
tions for two hours t
At the same time 150
ings, of a total of 400
Hooghly, a base barra
cutta, also staged a s
To-night the "st
Bombay said that the
pany of 60 men from a
Royal Indian Navy h
tained and some of t
been charged with m
"strikers" added tha
ary action had been ta
Indian ratings on ot
It appeared to-nigh
of the ships of the R
Navy in Bombay Ha
practically unman
orange, green and w
Congress flag flew fro
sweeper H.M.I.S. La
motor minesweeper.

The Royal Indian Navy mutiny as reported in the *Daily Telegraph* in February 1946.

year in the 1900s between 1600 and 2300 men attempted to desert their ships. As conditions improved on the Navy's battleships and cruisers in the 1920s and 1930s this rate dropped by 90 per cent, but it remained high among merchant seamen, who continued to suffer the worst hardships. Desertion from cargo ships remained a fairly routine occurrence during the inter-war years, and it actually increased during the Second World War. In 1942 there were 1850 cases and in 1943, 1420. The most popular places for desertion were American and Australian ports – and the majority who deserted were never caught.

Drink and a good time ashore were the great consolations for those who worked at sea, but if they got out of control these too could develop into mutinous behaviour. The amount of shore leave granted by the captain and the amount of money advanced to the men to spend in port were two major bones of contention. If the crew thought they were being short-changed they would frequently take what they felt was due to them. Paint, rope, cigarettes or even some of the cargo itself would be sold to pay for beer money ashore. They would also return to the ship late, more often than not returning drunk. Predictably, almost two-thirds of all recorded offences in the merchant navy were 'absence without leave'. The ratings were often fined a day's pay, or worse, but some captains turned a blind eye to this kind of misdemeanour to win the goodwill of the crew. Very occasionally a crew might mutiny and take the ship into port to have a good time. Peter Irvine remembers one such incident that occurred on a North Sea trawler at Christmas 1958.

'We were steaming off the Norway coast and we broke into the ship's bond – we stole twelve bottles of rum and got drunk on them. This was where the mutiny started. We wanted some more, wanted an excuse to get into port, so we went into the galley and threw all the tops of the stove over the side so there was no way to cook. So the skipper had to put into port in Norway and we were selling all the gear from the ship to buy whisky. We went on a real drunken spree. We were arrested over there and fined, then they brought us home and when we anchored off the Humber they took us into police custody. Five of us got sentenced to six months in jail and I remember the headline in the *Hull Daily Mail* was "Five Hull Seamen Sentenced for Mutiny on the High Seas".'

Those seafarers who suffered the worst conditions and the most exploitation were undoubtedly the Indians, Chinese, Africans and Arabs who together made up around one-third of the labour force of the merchant fleet in the 1930s. They were recruited as cheap labour and were generally paid only a quarter to a half of the wages earned by British seamen. Most had a reputation for hard work and obedience to authority. Many were employed as firemen in the engine room, a job for which they were thought to be well suited because they could cope with the intense heat. Until the Second World War the reputation of 'foreign' seamen for amenability was well founded – they had little choice, facing dismissal or even deportation if they did not comply with their lot. But all this would change with the coming of war in 1939, for many seamen from across the Empire did not regard it as 'their' war and would no longer tolerate the old inequalities and racist attitudes. If they were to risk their lives in war – and many were among the high wartime casualty figures for merchant seamen – they expected better treatment. From 1939 on there was an unprecedented wave of strikes and protests by Indian, African and Chinese seamen for improved pay and conditions. The first response of the authorities was to severely fine or imprison entire 'foreign' crews who refused to sail. But the increased bargaining power of such crews enabled them to win substantial improvements during the course of the war. By 1942, for example, the Ellerman Line was paying 'foreign' seamen wages that were 200 per cent more than their pre-war level.

The most formidable naval mutiny to affect Britain and her Empire was that of the Royal Indian Navy in February 1946. This had expanded considerably during the war to 28,000 men, but many of its British officers – some of them former tea planters from Ceylon and Malaya – were unfit to command. High-handed and racist treatment of Indian crews throughout the war combined with poor working conditions and low pay to create an explosive situation. The mutiny began in Bombay on 17 February at a naval training school, as Admiral Charles Nanda remembers. News of the incident spread quickly and in the next few days, on a wave of nationalist feeling, 10,000 ratings and 56 ships mutinied. The rising was brutally suppressed in the subsequent weeks, with over 200 mutineers killed. Less than 18 months after the mutiny India received its independence and those mutineers still in prison were released. It was the bloodiest insurrection experienced by the British armed forces since the naval mutinies at the end of the eighteenth century – and the dismantling of the British Empire after the war ensured that it would be the last.

BILL GLENTON

Bill looks far younger than his 70 years. Confident and relaxed, he enjoys showing visitors around his beautifully restored vicarage home in northeast Yorkshire, the reward for a lifetime's work as a journalist, author and travel writer. In August 1944, as a

naïve 18-year-old naval conscript, he found himself involved in one of the great forgotten mutinies on board HMS *Lothian*, an Admiral's flagship, at Balboa in Panama. After the war Bill returned to Fleet Street. He lives with Ann, his second wife, whom he married in 1976. He has three children by his first wife.

Before I joined the Navy when I was a teenager I had the typical impression of what a mutiny was and what mutineers were. There were goodies and baddies. And the goodies were the officers and the baddies were the men! This is what one gleaned from having seen *Mutiny on the Bounty* and read various books on naval mutinies. It was only when I got involved in one myself that I realized how wrong that concept really was.

Well, I completed my initial training and I ended up in Devonport barracks awaiting a draft ... we all hoped for a very nice draft, particularly away from a war zone or at least in a decent ship. And then one day the drafting Master at Arms came round and we were called out, several score of us, and told we were going to some vessel we'd never even heard of – HMS *Lothian*. What on earth is she? I mean, she didn't feature among well-known ships of the Royal Navy and so it was all a bit of a mystery to us, but at least we were glad to get away from Devonport barracks, which was a hell of a place to be in. So we looked forward to getting to this ship, which was lying in Greenock. But when we eventually got there we were absolutely aghast. I mean she was a real mishmash of a ship. She was obviously a cargo liner which had been converted and they'd stuck bits and pieces on all over... a gun fore and aft. Of course the worst possible impression we had was of the mess deck itself. There was hardly any ventilation. She was literally a steel box into which they packed about a hundred seamen and she was absolutely jammed tight like sardines in a tin. It was absolutely putrid down there. It was hot, smelly, and of course you had seamen smoking all the time. You had wet

Bill Glenton in 1945, a year after sailing from Greenock with 'Force X'.

clothing… you had everything that made life unbearable. And so really, for new entries like we were, and we were all about 18 or 19, it was a bit of a shock, this being more or less our first ship in the Royal Navy.

We didn't even know where we were going. We eventually set sail from Greenock and we were all pretty seasick. I suppose we were halfway across the Atlantic before we got our sea legs. Then we were told we were going to the Pacific and that we were to take part in the invasion of the Philippines. Well, that came as a complete shock to us 'cos as far as we were concerned there was only one war that mattered and that was the war in Europe and the war in the Pacific was purely an American affair from our point of view. And so we sort of looked upon that rather begrudgingly if you like, because although America was our ally we weren't that keen to go all the way to the Pacific in the conditions which we were suffering.

And as we got south, of course – as we sailed from New York and it got hotter and hotter – conditions in the mess deck became virtually totally unbearable. We had rats, thousands of cockroaches, weevils in the food… and the food was bad and inadequate enough as it was. The water we had to drink was foul. Then there was the intense heat and the putrid, fetid atmosphere in the mess deck. I remember how exhausted I felt. I was virtually physically drained of all energy – the conditions had totally run us down. We couldn't go on living a tough naval existence without good food.

Well, we got to Panama, and I think that was the crunch point. The ringleaders – as they turned out to be – started saying to us, 'Well, we've got to do something about it, we mustn't go any further, we're not going to sail across the Pacific until the Navy does something about this'. And although as young matelots we were very nervous about even the *word* 'mutiny', we knew that they were talking a lot of sense, that we could see ourselves becoming so physically incapable that we would never be able to finish the voyage except in a canvas bag and being pushed over the side. That might sound dramatic, but at the time it didn't sound so dramatic, it sounded a distinct possibility. We were all very sick.

We were lying alongside in Balboa having just come through the Panama Canal and that evening these half-a-dozen ringleaders went round all the messes saying, 'All right lads, tomorrow morning we refuse to take the ship to sea. Now when the pipe to take the ship to sea comes, you just sit tight in the mess decks.' And it was agreed that this would happen at mid-morning break, which was around about 10.30. Well, they piped, and we did nothing.

We sat there, sort of looking at each other with a cold, nervous half-grin on our faces, hoping that perhaps a miracle would happen and the captain would come down and say 'Sorry boys, all is forgiven, we'll do something about it', but of course that never happened. The chief petty officer was aghast and warned us that unless we came out and started work we were in the most serious trouble.

But there was a terrific sense of solidarity. In fact I remember at one time we all started singing a rather bawdy version of the *Red Flag*, I think more to cheer us up than anything, you know. I think – if I remember the words – it was 'The working class can kiss my ass, I've got the jaunty's job at last', the jaunty being the Master at Arms. And we sang a few songs and we tried to keep ourselves happy. But the conditions got so bad down below that one of the ringleaders decided we couldn't stay down there any longer so he went up and knocked on the hatch, which had been put down on us, and yelled that we wanted to come out. Now whether they thought that we were giving in or not I don't know, but they opened up the hatch and before they had a chance to change their minds there was one mad rush – everybody dashed up on deck, we were desperate to get out of that mess deck at any cost and there was this stampede to get out on deck. And there were these armed marines... it was such a stampede of matelots that we almost knocked the marines over.

We stayed there for a bit; it wasn't the sort of violent mutiny that you might imagine, we were just standing around. Then it was decided that we should go ashore and leave the ship, so we went down the gangway on to the quayside. And there was a big crowd there by now, mostly American seamen, and they were jeering and cheering and catcalling – they were obviously finding the whole thing very funny. Which was of course a total embarrassment for the Admiral and the Captain on board. Because while the mutiny was taking place they were actually holding lunch for the American naval officers in Balboa and they had the embarrassment of trying to get them ashore without knowing there was a mutiny on board! And I don't think they were very successful either 'cos no sooner had they stepped down the gangway than they could see us standing there.

I think we half expected the Admiral to send the marines ashore to bring us back on board, but to our astonishment who should appear down the gangway but the Army contingent, clutching their rifles – and I may say now that they looked extremely nervous about it. They obviously were very reluctant to do this. Anyway, their captain lined them up in front of us and stepped forward and told us that unless we returned aboard he would be forced to take action. Well, we'd always regarded – in typical ratings fashion – the army as a bit of a joke, so it wasn't surprising that we started to jeer at them and laugh at them, which made them even more uncomfortable I think, and then one or two of the bolder mutineers stepped forward and tried to grab rifles off the soldiers. Well, things were obviously going to get out of hand because the captain was clearly not going to give the order for them to fire at us or anything like that. And they clearly weren't going to be in a capable situation to arrest us, so he suddenly called them together, lined them up and marched them back aboard like the Duke of York.

Anyway, it seemed that we weren't going to gain anything from our actions so eventually most of us went back on board – we left the ringleaders on the quay. They were locked up and given hard labour. I suppose most of the seamen got off very lightly. All we got was 'three months two and two', which means second class for conduct and second class for leave. That meant we had to do extra drills and duties every day for three months and we didn't go ashore in all that time.

But you really grasped how horrible the conditions had been and appreciated the full consequences of them when we eventually got to Australia two or three months later. Because sixty per cent of the seamen were taken ashore to hospital with TB. Myself, I'd lost a considerable amount of weight. In fact, I was down to six and a half stone [41.3 kilograms], and I don't think I was exceptional aboard that ship.

BILL HART

Bill lives on a boat on the Grand Union Canal near Milton Keynes, Buckinghamshire. He was born in 1922, the son of a Liverpool merchant seaman. A short, stocky man with a huge white beard, Bill loves nothing better than to talk about his days in the merchant navy, which began in 1937 and ended in 1955 when he was banned from British ships. He was a rebel, angered by the appalling conditions which the merchant seamen were forced to endure. He was one of the founders of the Seafarers' Rank and File Committee and a leader in the unofficial 1947 strike that paved the way for a better deal for seamen. After leaving the sea, Bill became a construction engineer. He retired in 1982 although he still works part-time for an engineering company.

Well, the nearest thing you can get to a ship's stokehold is Dante's *Inferno*. The average cargo boat has nine fires in three boilers. Each fireman is responsible for looking after three fires. When you first come on watch one fire's got to be cleaned, raked over to the side and then all the hot ashes pulled out. Then you rake it back over and pull the rest of the ashes out. So it's heat and steam – working in these conditions is really exhausting. You need a very heavy singlet to soak up the sweat, which pours out of the lace holes on your dungarees. They used to wear what is always known in Liverpool as 'bow-yanks', and you used to put them round your trousers to keep the weight of the dungarees – which are soaked in sweat – from being too heavy on your legs. Now the average boiler usually blows off about 210 pounds per square inch, so you've got a line there which is known as 'the blood', and the object of the exercise is to keep that needle on the blood all the while to give maximum steam to the engine. Imagine doing a watch when you're covered in coal dust, you're filthy dirty and exhausted. To get cleaned up every fireman was supplied with a bucket, a sweat rag and a bar of soap – and water, of course, was rationed in ships. You went into an open wash place – and in the depths of winter it was freezing cold – and you used that bucket of water to wash yer hair, to wash yer face, wash yer whole body down, and finally, with what was left in the bucket, tip it over yourself to rinse yourself off. They were the conditions that British seamen suffered after four hours' hard steaming in a coal-burning ship. Other facilities, like the toilet – well there was one toilet, made of cast iron, that after a while was rusty as hell and stinking to high heaven. Inside the fo'c'sle you got all the water coming in as she shipped seas, so conditions were constantly wet. If you were housed aft you had the constant chatter and noise of the steering gear, which was housed above. Between May and October there was no heating and there was no running water. The food in nine cases out of ten, apart from certain companies, was absolutely disgusting and used to be dished up in metal dixies.

Most shipping companies had names based on some hungry aspect of the company's reputation. There was 'Hungry Hogarths', and Harrisons were known as 'Two of fat and one of lean' because of their poor meat. When you loaded with potatoes they went into the spud locker. The spuds stank to high heaven and weren't really eatable.

Most of the complaints aboard a ship that I can remember of those days were nearly always about food. A tin of condensed milk had to last three weeks. No fresh milk or powdered milk. You got a bar of soap – for the down-below crowd – once a week. That was supposed to wash you, wash all your gear and whatever. I think the real test of going away to sea was whether you could tolerate those conditions. People were very reluctant to stand up in front and be the spokesman. They were afraid of repercussions, but the usual drill was to go to the Chief Steward first. You'd get the same meal, curry and rice, served up again, cold, unappetizing, stinking, and you knew it was stale meat. So you'd march up to the Skipper and he'd say, 'What's the matter with the food? It's only the same as I'm having', which was a lie because he was probably having lamb chops. And he always went through the drill of tasting because you'd be carrying the grub in front of you, saying would you eat this? – it's a big tin dixie with all this slop in. He'd take a spoon and say 'Absolutely first class'. So you either did one of two things: you put it over his bloody head or you walked off calling him all the bastards under the sun. But there was nothing you could really do. You got it off your chest but you didn't achieve anything and you'd blackened yer name because they'd let you know as you were getting near the home port that you wouldn't be required on the next voyage. Oh, they'd make life difficult for you. If a crew were moaning about the food, as soon as you arrived in port and you looked for a sub so you could go ashore there'd be no sub list, or they'd give you such a small amount you couldn't go anywhere. So all the while they had control. If you considered any direct action, like refusing to go on watch, the consequences were a very severe flogging, firing, or prosecution. You couldn't change it.

I remember once tipping the food over the cook's head because it was so bad. Occasionally the skipper or the engineer were hit, but they had to have the proof of it and if yer mates were sound and solid they kept quiet. Many an engineer been belted down below and many a skipper been belted in the quietude of his own room. I hit a skipper once during the war, in the *Ocean Gypsy* on our way home from West Africa, and there was a young lad, Ginger, who'd had a message that his father had died. He was only about nineteen or twenty. He was terribly upset and took ill. We demanded that the skipper put him in 'hospital'. Now a hospital in a cargo boat is only a room with a separate swinging bed. It took about three visits to the skipper and threats before we got him moved. The lad's weight was going down – it was obvious he was seriously ill – but the skipper said he was a bloody malcontent and if he didn't get out of his bunk soon he'd stop his wages. In the convoy was a destroyer, HMS *Devonshire*, who had a doctor, and we asked the skipper to send to the *Devonshire* whether they'd put a doctor aboard or whether they'd put Ginger aboard the *Devonshire* so he could be properly looked after. Anyway, nothing happened. We finally arrived in Liverpool and sent for the doctor. The next day he died in Walton

Hospital from blackwater fever and I went straight up to the skipper. I told him 'You bloody murdering bastard', and I thumped him then. I didn't only thump him once, I knocked him all round his bloody cabin. That lad's life could have been saved, but that was the attitude at sea and that's what annoyed and inflamed people. And it cost me in the long run – it cost me £26.00, which was the equivalent of a month's pay.

One thing that got better during the war was the money. They had to pay us a bit more because they needed us more ... Then on VE Day, 1945, I was in the MV *Geordic* in Naples and the second engineer – putting his head inside the doorway – said, 'Well the war's over now, you bastards won't have it all your own way now. We're back to the old days. From now on you'll ask for your bloody jobs.'

Now, the thing that triggered the 1947 strike was the cut in pay. They took the war bonus off, which meant a big cut in pay. By the end of 1945 they were talking about reducing the wages. There were plenty of seamen available, and people who'd spent the whole war at sea were denied the right to join another ship. There were factors which pointed to them getting back to the old days, so we organized a series of meetings. I was chairman of the strike committee. I convened in various ports throughout Great Britain and also overseas. We formed an organization that could challenge the National Union of Seamen, who seemed a willing party to all the reforms that were taking place to the shipowners' advantage and not to ours. So that leads to the 1947 Seamen's Strike. A lot of work had gone on informing people by word of mouth. It was a tramping from port to port, taking every opportunity that arose. If a concert was held in the seamen's mission we'd take over the stage and get our message across.

In Liverpool we called this meeting, we got the enthusiasm of the seamen and we raised enough money to book Picton Hall. When we saw the attendance at Picton Hall we realized the feeling was sound and strong and we were echoing the feelings of the seamen. The last meeting we called before the strike was at the Liverpool Stadium. We filled it to overflowing and then we knew the strength of feeling and that the seamen were prepared to go all the way. In between the meetings we used to go aboard ships, meet the crews and get pledges from them. So we took the decision to call a strike for the 26th October, which was a Saturday morning. The pledges were such that the whole port of Liverpool would come to a standstill, and it did.

Seamen always had this dream of a strike. People always said you can't organize seamen because they're never all together, they're scattered all over the world. Also, the punishment for getting involved was so harsh.

There was a stage during the strike when I lost my voice completely. We'd do maybe thirty, forty meetings a day, addressing everyone – outside pubs, on lemonade boxes and beer crates, on the dock road against the noise of the traffic – talking to the dockers, the seamen, the ship repair workers, the lock gate men, tugboat men, all of them. I'd be telling them the sacrifice that we made during the war, the conditions that we put up with, the impudence of the shipowners in trying to reduce our wages. And I always told them there's forty-five thousand of our number that's never going to come back – we'd been lucky, we'd survived the war and we had a responsibility now. That was the one thing that seamen always respected and understood, that they had a moral responsibility, not just an economic responsibility, to make conditions better.

Now we ran that strike on one public telephone box. The only means of communication was our committee rooms in Scotland Road, with a telephone box below – and that telephone box was sacrosanct. People in the vicinity wouldn't use the box. If they saw a stranger go to use it they'd say, 'You can't use that box, that's the Seamen's box'. One day we got a telephone call from London, from Barney Flynn, saying it was true that there was a trainload of scabs leaving Euston station to man the *Empress of Scotland*. We told Barney and two other lads to board the train till they arrived at Lime Street, and we would meet the train at Lime Street with a crowd of pickets. When the train arrived Barney said that the carriages had been shunted off. We met a railwayman and he said they were taking them to the Riverside station, so we got all the pickets together and said 'Make your way down to Riverside station, but go in twos and threes, don't make it obvious'. We managed to get about sixty or seventy people down there and you can imagine the Dock Road – night time, winter's night, tungsten lights and the orange glare and we're waiting for this train. By this time the number of pickets had grown – word of mouth had got round that something big was taking place in the Dock Road. There were about 120 men. And the gates of the siding opened and the engine began to appear and everyone shouted 'Down to the railway lines'. So we lay across the lines, determined not to let the train pass. I can still see the train driver's cab and his face was stark white in an absolute state of shock, jamming everything on and shutting the engine down and the perspiration pouring down his face and he said 'I want no part of this'. He started moving the train back.

Soon the police arrived. The next minute the Dock Road is snowing with police. Well, I suppose the police were trained in those days in one particular way – they're either with us or agin us. And if they're agin us it's batons out, and so it was a battle.

We eventually negotiated with the police and things calmed down. Following this negotiations took place and a settlement was offered for returning to work. The first we knew that they were going to renege on the deal was when the police arrived at the committee rooms and arrested me and charged me with conspiracy. I was arrested for conspiracy to prevent people doing what they had a legal right to do and conspiracy to break the Merchant Shipping Act and then with conspiracy to cause violence. We stood trial in the January of 1948 and it lasted nine days. I got six months. To my mind it was just to teach us a lesson, sort of hitting back at people who'd dared to defy the establishment and defy the shipping companies.

TERRI GARDNER

Always the entertainer, the lounge of Terri's flat in Barking, east London, is dominated by a stunning portrait of him in drag. He is more than happy to talk about his many years as a performer, whether it was as a sophisticated cabaret artiste or a pantomime dame. Yet he becomes more reflective when asked about his experience as a homosexual in the Royal Navy during the last war. Born in 1920, Terri came to terms with his sexuality early on and settled happily into his life as a 'theatrical'. But his conscription into the Navy in 1940 meant being plunged into a secret, illicit world, and he was targeted and eventually discharged for being gay. Terri is still very active in the theatre. 'There is nothing greater in the world than being able to entertain people,' he says.

Terri Gardner joins the Royal Navy in 1940.

When it came to being called up I actually chose to go into the Navy. I was picked to be a cook. It was exciting, the idea of being surrounded by all these butch men, but it was frightening too because I had no idea what my life would be like. A gay person who I knew at the time said they might give me a bad time and that the best way for me to be was downright outrageous.

I'd been a pro entertainer who was just getting my foothold in the theatre and music hall when I went in, so I had that little bit of experience. So naturally I went to find out who was in charge of entertainment wherever I was and got in and did some shows, which made things very much easier for me. Well, in the bottom of the kit bag I always carried round a wig and a dress and a bit of make-up so that I knew that within minutes I could transform myself and become an entertainer. I suppose in a way the wig and costume were a complete disguise. Being young and being rather pretty I found I could get away with murder… and did, frequently.

I've always believed in making people laugh. If you make people laugh they automatically… they're on your side to start with. I just went on and told some rather risqué stories and sang in my rather peculiar voice. I suppose, well, during the war of course it was very different because the troops, when they were massed together, thousands of men, all at a loose end, entertainment meant a great deal to them. I had to take a few kicks, of course; not everybody likes theatrical people, or gay people, but funnily enough I don't even remember running into real unpleasantness the whole time I was in the services.

I decided the time had come where I should see a bit of action and volunteered to serve on a ship. Of course, little did I know what I was letting myself in for. On the corvette that I was drafted to we used to run from Liverpool to Gibraltar, which in those days used to take maybe as long as fourteen days because we had to be off the shipping lanes.

One was young, and sex is very much a thing in your life when you're in your twenties – you're out to get every bit and have as much fun as you possibly can. The married man away from home and in the Navy, as far as I could see, was the worst sort of man – he would go out of his way for a bit of nonsense. The difficulties were finding somewhere to be intimate. One place was behind the weatherproof curtains on the weather side of the ship because nobody could use those doors to come in on you and no one went out that side because they were all afraid of being swept overboard. One had to be a bit discrete with affairs because, quite apart from it being a punishable offence, you couldn't let everybody know what was going on.

We used to have a night ashore and stop ashore in those days. There was a part of Chatham where all the women let out beds to sailors – for one-and-six [7.5 pence] a night I think it was – so if one of the boys said 'Shall we have a run ashore tonight?', the first thing we'd do was book a bed. During the many air raids one had to go down to the

Terri Gardner in full drag in the early 1950s. After leaving the Royal Navy, Terri had a successful career in the theatre.

shelters, and I found that everything was going on down there.

I was absolutely surrounded by men and by temptation and this went on until I just couldn't take any more of it. I became very unhappy about my life and became mentally disarranged – life was just too difficult and I was having dreadful dreams. I suppose for the only time ever in my life suicide entered my head.

I went to see a naval psychologist and he told me he thought I was homosexual and I was reported. I never set sail on the corvette again. One of the most amazing periods of my life was when I was awaiting my discharge. I was under 'open arrest', they called it, because I hadn't actually done anything wrong but I was homosexual. I found out later on that there had been a court of inquiry on the corvette and everyone was sort of questioned about their relationship with me. They were trying to get someone to admit to having sexual intercourse with me and then a prison sentence would follow. Fortunately no one spoke against me. I found open arrest absolutely awful. I had nothing to do all day or night and time became endless. At times I used to think I was going out of my mind. I know I used to count the bricks in the wall. Eventually I was given this 'dishonourable' discharge and thrown out – they said 'Away you go'.

Although I felt ashamed to be discharged dishonourably, it didn't make any difference to my life at all. No one ever saw the note and my father was so happy to see me home, knowing I wasn't going away again. It certainly has not affected my life at all.

ALAN LAWTON

Alan was born in 1925 in the deep-sea fishing community of Hessle Road, Hull, the son of a shipbroker. He is a sensitive and thoughtful man who has reflected much on his involvement in the mutiny on a minesweeper in 1944. A former office clerk, he had volunteered for the Royal Navy two years before. His attempt on the life of his lieutenant commander went undetected, and in the post-war years he emigrated to Australia. When he talks of the mutiny he is still filled with emotion, reliving the trauma of what was probably the most dramatic moment of his life. Alan returned to Hull in 1981 and settled down with his second wife, Rose. He has three children from his first marriage.

I volunteered for the Navy at 17 and, after an examination in Hull, I was shipped down to Devonport. The attitude of the men on the lower deck depended entirely on the officers. The first lieutenant, who is called 'Jimmie the One', he's the one who is supposed to look after you. Our 'Jimmie the One' was, I think, a bank manager and Royal Navy reserve, which meant that he knew very little about seamanship – and a minesweeper is full of seamanship.

I was put on the mine-sweeping party… about six of us. Putting out the 'sweep' is a highly dangerous, skilled job and the man in the lead is in most danger – as the mines pop up you have to dodge them.

Our Jimmie was very inefficient, he didn't know how to do the job. The mines were very dodgy things and would blow up for the least blink of an eyelid. Our first lieutenant came out from underneath the depth-charge racks, where he was protected. As soon as a mine blew up he was protected by the steel. Quite often there were mines tangled up in the gear or jammed. Once a mine drifted off and blew up. It didn't damage the ship much but one of the chaps in front was hit in the neck with a large lump of red-hot shrapnel and he was nearly decapitated. The first lieutenant came back to the quarterdeck and I just called him every name under the sun. I was immediately put down into the tiller flap, sort of under arrest, although I was released later because they were short of men. That was when we decided something had to be done – that was the beginning of our plan. We must get rid of this officer before he kills someone. He was incompetent to the point of being dangerous to the rest of us in the mine-sweeping party. When a man doesn't take precautions to ensure the safety of his team and accidents happen – like the man whose hands were cut off and the man caught up in a wire – you have to act.

Alan Lawton, aged 17, just before he was posted to his first minesweeper.

Well, we used to stop sweeping at night and four of us that night went down to the lower mess deck into a corner on our own and we said we'd got to get rid of this man. One man said it's no use talking to the captain, he won't listen to us, and a little fellow who worked on the quarterdeck with us said 'Let's do him in'. Simple as that. I was doubtful because I thought, this is taking someone else's life, but we discussed it for at least an hour. Eventually we decided that there was nothing else to do and he was going to kill somebody if we didn't act. The little man said 'We'll shove him over the side when we're moving'.

That's when we decided to have four cigarette butts of different sizes in matchboxes – the ones with the shortest were the ones that pushed him over. We shuffled the matchboxes round the table, on the mess-deck table, and each one of us took one and we opened them all together, in front of each other, and the two shortest ones were the first ones to have a go. I was the shortest, actually, and I would be a liar if I said I wasn't scared – because I was and I think we all were really. When I realized that I had the short one I was quite frightened, and the fact that it wasn't done straight away – you had to think about it in your hammock at night – made it even worse and everybody's eyes were on you so the stress of that was quite horrific really.

We chose a time when the sweep was nearly in – in other words we weren't in full swing but we were moving fairly quickly. The man that was at work with me on this watched carefully and when 'Jimmie the One' came out from his hiding-place as usual and he went down to the sloping end of the depth-charge rack, which was very wet, he had one hand on a davit, peering over the side… and I looked at my mate and he looked at me and we just jumped on to the top of the depth-charge rack, walked quickly down, put our hands on his back and pushed. I can still hear him scream as he went over.

It was a strange feeling. I didn't want to let the other man down and he didn't want to let me down, but even at that stage I think we doubted whether we'd do it. I can still feel with my fingers… I can still feel the cloth of his uniform, but I hated him so much that we just pushed together. When he went over we jumped off the racks and just stood back and thought, this is it, we're going to get hung, drawn and quartered. But there was such a lot of confusion – boat hooks everywhere and ropes going over and so forth – that we stood back and nobody actually could prove that we did it because they didn't see us.

I think when we went down below some time afterwards we began to shake, both of us did, and somebody brought out the old bottle of rum and calmed us down, but I think we were shaking, and nothing happened until the second time. That was two other men and it was just a different position where he went over. I had sleepless nights, and I think the other chap did too. You see, nothing was said – nobody said we saw you push him over or you're going to be court-martialled. You see, in the Navy many crimes are punishable by death. We were in a state of anxiety for a long time. Then the name for rumour in the Navy is 'buzz' and the buzz went round the ship like wild fire that Jimmy the One was leaving. We were in port and he got to the bottom of the gangway with his bag and a big cheer went up. We had a big celebration that night. We'd won a small victory.

ADMIRAL SARDARILAL 'CHARLES' NANDA

Charles was born into a middle-class family at Gujranwala, now part of Pakistan, in 1915. His father worked for the Port Trust at Karachi. He joined the Royal Indian Navy as a volunteer reserve officer in 1940. In early 1946 he was teaching at the Signals School in Bombay, which was to become the flash point for the naval mutiny that followed. Charles married Sumitra in 1936 and they had three children. In 1970 he was appointed Chief of Staff for the Indian Navy, the highest position in the service. A highly intelligent and charming man, Charles is now retired and divides his time between homes in Delhi and London.

What triggered off the whole thing was the fact that the British commanding officer, Commander King, was walking round the mess decks where about five or six sailors were sitting and having their lunch. And he walked through the mess decks and these sailors continued with their lunch. So he stopped them and abused them and called them bastards. And put them on charge for not getting up and saluting him or paying him the respect that was due to a commanding officer. Now, normally speaking, on a mess deck when you're having your meals... I mean, this sort of thing was not done in the Signals School. So I think he overdid it, this thing, and put these boys on charge and they were punished.

But they thought their punishment was unjust and they were much aggrieved. Now during this period when this episode was going on there was a lot of talk in the Signals School barracks amongst the young sailors and one morning when they went for their breakfast they refused to eat it. In those days they used to get lentils – which are 'dhal' in the Indian language – they were given dhal and bread. Now some sailors got up – the officer of the day was walking around the mess decks – and they got up and they said 'Sir, this dhal is inedible, it's badly cooked and there's stones in it; we cannot eat this'. And they all refused to eat their food and walked out of the mess decks.

Now all the boys had gathered in groups all round the Signals School and work normally started at nine o'clock. So all the other officers, including myself, we came in to the Signals School about ten minutes to nine and we found that everybody was wandering around, so we asked somebody what's happening – is there a holiday today or something? Nobody is in proper uniform, they were all wandering around the barracks and some boys, you know, sort of laughed and they said 'No Sir, we've gone on strike'. Eventually we discovered that it was a resentment against the treatment that was given by the commanding officer to these sailors.

I was one of the senior Indian officers there and we held an urgent meeting with a number of the sailors to discuss their grievances. But by this time they were quite agitated and they had produced a written charter of demands. One of them was that Commander King should apologize. Well, when we told him this he said 'This is rubbish, they must go back on duty', and unfortunately this didn't help matters at all.

In the meantime the communications ratings who were housed in the Signals School barracks put on a tape on the Indian naval broadcast – which is going to all the ships and establishments of the Indian Navy – to say that the Signals School was on strike and requested that they should all go on strike, which they did do. The signal had been regularly transmitted on ticker tape all the time and the word was going around all the mess decks or the galleys to all the sailors without the knowledge of the officers. So the sailors knew more about what was happening than the officers knew. And there was a great deal of anti-British feeling. You see, during the war a large number of British civilians – tea planters, people like that – had become officers in the Royal Indian Navy, and this led to a certain amount of resentment with the sailors. They were being treated as masters and slaves – let's put it frankly like that.

Then, when all this was happening, there were rumours that the Royal Navy was being sent for to deal with the mutiny and it was going to bombard Bombay. That aroused the passions of everybody in the streets, who said 'What the hell, why should we be butchered like this? If the Royal Navy is going to put us down we'll do something about it.' And that caused a lot of riots in the city itself. There were large crowds on the streets, slogan-shouting – 'British quit India', this sort of thing and there was shooting too, with a lot of people killed.

And there I was in Bombay.... The sailors who had mutinied were fêted and treated as heroes – they were the ones who had the guts to stand up to the British. They didn't see it so much as mutiny but as an expression of feeling against the British. The British had promised self-rule and there was a feeling, rightly or wrongly, that we were being cheated again – it was all taking too long now that the war was over. I think that the mutiny did help the independence movement. I think it created a feeling that there may be another mutiny like the 1857 Mutiny where a lot of British lives would be lost and that the British could not defend their citizens in India. Therefore the best thing would be to get rid of it and give independence.

4

Sailors at War

Britain entered the Second World War with an awesome reputation for its sea power. The Royal Navy had reigned supreme since the days of Nelson and the Napoleonic Wars – or so it seemed. At the outset of hostilities newspapers and newsreels trumpeted this faith in the fleet as the ultimate defender of Britain and her empire. But the confident rhetoric hid a growing awareness of naval decline both in the Admiralty and in the Government itself. In September 1939 Britain was not the unrivalled sea power she had once been. The Royal Navy had only just survived the First World War with its reputation intact and since then economic recession had brought a series of savage spending cuts that depleted the ships and manpower at the command of the Sea Lords. Archaic tactical ideas – in particular a belief in the battleship as a key strategic weapon in any future conflict – left the Royal Navy extremely vulnerable to enemy attack.

The Navy's main role in the last war was to keep open the sea routes to Britain from the outside world, just as it had done in the First World War. As an island-based imperial power, Britain's military and economic strength depended on her ability to import food, oil and raw materials in enormous quantities. This import trade was largely carried by Britain's merchant fleet of around 3000 ocean-going ships – the largest in the world. Germany had long planned to target this cargo-carrying fleet, and by investing heavily in a U-boat building programme it hoped to cripple Britain's war economy. The defeat of France in June 1940 put this within Germany's grasp as the French Atlantic ports fell into the

hands of Admiral Dönitz, to be used as a front line for U-boat operations. Heavy losses of destroyers in the Dunkirk evacuation meant that there were few escort vessels left to protect British convoys across the Atlantic and to the Empire. The alarming consequence was that between June and September 1940 U-boats sank 274 ships for the loss of only two of their own. By early 1941, 400 ships had been sunk in the previous eight months. The worst month was November 1942, when 119 ships went down in the Atlantic – partly as a result of the adoption of the 'wolf pack' system in which U-boats concentrated large numbers against a single convoy in order to overwhelm the escort. The success of the U-boats and the threat of starvation for the British people promoted one of the greatest crises of the war for the Government, to which it responded by introducing more and more stringent rationing.

One of the ironies of what came to be known as the 'Battle of the Atlantic' was that the men who were in the front line and who suffered most in terms of death and injury were not regular Royal Navy personnel but merchant seamen and civilian volunteers and conscripts. The convoy escort crews were drawn mainly from 'hostilities only' seamen, who were conscripted from civilian life, and reserve or volunteer reserve naval officers, many of whom had never been to sea before. They faced extreme danger, with around 25,000 killed on escort duty during the course of the war. Yet they did their duty with extraordinary stoicism. A young crew member of one of the small corvette escort boats that were tossed around on the mountainous seas of the mid-Atlantic was Cyril Stephens.

'We never had a clue what the sea was all about. We were bookies, runners, chippies, bricklayers, painters, you know, and suddenly we're meant to be seamen. On our corvette I was always seasick, always for the first three days on a trip I was sick. It's one of the most unpleasant things there is in life – sometimes I wished to God I was dead. I think the best way to describe a corvette at sea is like a terrier and a rat. The sea would kind of get hold of you and shake you, you'd gradually go up on this big wave and look down and you'd think, oh crikey, and the next minute you'd be sliding down and into another big wave. Then you'd have three tons of water come over the top of you. And the U-boats, they were everywhere. We had to scour the horizon for them with our binoculars, but you could never spot one. Our officer used to say to us when we were

Left: **HMS *Benbow* in 1941. The Royal Navy had invested heavily in battleships rather than submarines and was ill-equipped to fight a modern naval war.**

Overleaf: **A British convoy crossing the Atlantic in April 1940. There were few escort vessels to protect these convoys and they suffered heavy losses between 1940 and 1943.**

on watch: "If you can spot a U-boat and sink it I'll see if I can get you a VC." But funnily enough, daft as it may seem, I had no fear. I couldn't even swim, but I honestly didn't have any fear at all.'

It was the merchant seamen who suffered most from the U-boat attacks. By the end of 1940, 6000 merchant seamen had been killed. Seven thousand more lost their lives in 1941 and 8000 in 1942. In total, more than 50,000 British merchant seamen died as a result of enemy action in the war. In the early years of the war little was done to alleviate their suffering – until 1941 a man's pay was stopped the moment his ship was sunk. For those who survived, the long journey home was unpaid – as Sidney Graham remembers.

Britain was essentially ill-equipped to fight a modern naval war. Much of her manpower and hardware were tied up in battleships and cruisers to be used in set-piece conflicts, which were never anywhere near as important as the Admiralty had imagined. The Navy had only a small and outdated submarine fleet which, in the first years of the war, was largely ineffective compared to the German U-boats. Captain Mervyn Wingfield recalls how difficult – and sometimes disastrous – it was fighting an underwater war against an enemy who was better trained and prepared and whose submarines were often superior in speed, range and firepower.

Air power also proved to be crucial in the war at sea, and again the Navy found itself at a serious disadvantage. The Fleet Air Arm, always a poor relation to the RAF and with limited resources, began the war with outdated aircraft like the Swordfish and just six aircraft carriers. Despite its old-fashioned appearance and slow speed, the Swordfish achieved good results in the hands of dedicated crews, who often viewed them with great affection. But casualties were very high and a large proportion of the older and more experienced crews lost their lives. The *Luftwaffe* was by far the most effective air force. Off Crete in April 1941, for example, the *Luftwaffe* sank three cruisers and six destroyers and seriously damaged two battleships, one aircraft carrier, six cruisers and seven destroyers, which represented the greater part of the Mediterranean fleet. They also terrorized the seamen who found themselves involved in the Battle of the Atlantic. Long-range German aircraft made a number of lethal bombing raids on merchant ships and were almost as much of a threat to the convoys as the U-boats. Commander Ronnie Hay remembers the disadvantages the Fleet Air Arm laboured under and how the immense stress could undermine morale and, ultimately, lead to the death of some battle-weary pilots.

In April 1942 Britain was losing the war at sea. The merchant fleet and the Royal Navy had borne the brunt of the worst years of the war for Britain. The

An Allied convoy comes under air attack in the North Sea, 1940. By the end of that year, 6000 British merchant seamen had lost their lives.

odds were stacked against them. Total losses for the Navy included four aircraft carriers, 16 cruisers, 78 destroyers and 44 submarines. Despite this, most of our interviewees recall a strong resilience in the face of defeat – losing was, for many, unimaginable. This attitude is vividly reflected in the memories of David Holmes, whose ambition from his early teens was to be 'the best gunner in the navy'. However, by mid-1942 the worst of the Navy's war was over. The losses would be significantly reduced until the war ended in August 1945.

The turning point came with the entry of the United States into the war in December 1941 after the Japanese bombing of its Pacific fleet at Pearl Harbour. America's immense military and manufacturing power would soon prove decisive. There was the mass production of 'liberty' cargo ships to replace those sunk by the enemy in the Atlantic convoys. American naval control in the Pacific enabled the overstretched Royal Navy to provide many more escort ships for the convoys and to organize support groups to come to the help of those attacked

by 'wolf packs'. The crews of the corvettes and destroyers began to enjoy far more success depth-charging their U-boat adversaries. And the American-produced VLR (very long range) Liberator bombers, capable of carrying a large payload of depth charges, were the first that could effectively track down and attack submarines in mid-ocean.

The increasing success of the convoy system was vividly demonstrated in the Arctic convoys that supplied arms and ammunition to Soviet Russia, which had been brought into the war by Hitler's invasion in the spring of 1941. These supplies were essential to the Russian war effort on the Eastern Front and so Germany was determined to cut them off. British merchant ships had to run the gauntlet to and from the northern Russian ports of Archangel and Murmansk along a route that was always within the reach of enemy air, surface-ship and U-boat bases in Norway. Added to this, crews had to contend with the ferocious violence of Arctic weather, with fog, ice and gales of unparalleled frequency and intensity. The accretions of ice could become so heavy that they occasionally caused ships to capsize. Each delivery of arms was an epic achievement.

But from 1943 on, when these convoys were heavily protected by escort vessels (usually including an aircraft carrier), losses dropped to almost nothing. The cost to the U-boats was very high – 32 were sunk in Arctic convoy operations, a ratio not far from one U-boat for each of the 39 merchant ships they sank. About four million tons of cargo was delivered to Russian ports, including more than 7000 aircraft, 5000 tanks and huge quantities of other armaments and ammunition.

There was a growing realization that a well-protected convoy could be more than a cautious defence – it was actually the best offensive weapon against the German submarines. In the second half of 1943 Admiral Dönitz's U-boats were finally driven back by convoy escorts and long-range aircraft assisted by new radar equipment. The Allies were able to inflict huge losses on them and, by the beginning of 1944, they had ceased to be a menace to shipping. The Battle of the Atlantic had effectively been won. Of the 40,000 men who served in U-boats in the course of the war, 32,000 went down with their craft. This casualty rate of 80 per cent was the highest of any branch of any service in all the warring nations.

D-Day on 6 June 1944 was the ultimate reward for this hard-earned victory over the U-boat. Germany no longer possessed a fleet capable of posing a serious

The engine room of a British submarine. The Royal Navy had a small outdated submarine fleet which was largely ineffective compared to the German U-Boat.

Above: **The Fleet Air Arm in action on HMS *Indomitable*. Despite outdated aircraft, they achieved good results in the hands of dedicated crews.**

Overleaf: **A Kamikaze attack in 1945. Japan sent 1200 pilots on suicide missions to crash land on the ships of the Pacific Fleet.**

threat to the plan to invade France and create a second front. D-Day was the greatest amphibious operation the world has ever seen – its execution was a masterpiece of military planning and a great success for the Navy. The Royal Marines – the sea soldiers – were to play a key role in the invasion. Spearheading the assault were Royal Navy commandos, who had received intensive training for the operation. Their principal tasks were to secure the beachhead in the teeth of enemy defensive fire and to direct and control the arrival of successive waves of the landing craft that were bringing ashore the main body of fighting troops and their equipment. Altogether, 17,000 marines took part in the invasion, many in landing craft, in beach-control parties or manning the guns of the fleet. Although successful, there were heavy losses – with as many as half the men killed in some units. Stan Blacker still vividly recalls the drama of the landings under fire on the beaches of Normandy.

In the last years of the war Allied domination enabled the Royal Navy to enjoy its finest hour. Its submarines sank large amounts of Japanese shipping, which never adopted the protective measure of the convoy system. The Japanese mercantile marine lost 108,000 officers and men killed or missing during the war. The Fleet Air Arm too had by now grown into a powerful strategic weapon as large as the pre-war RAF in terms of its front-line aircraft. By 1945 it possessed 50 aircraft carriers of various types and several thousand aircraft.

But it was the United States that remained the dominant force. Its power was vividly demonstrated in the final sea battles of the war, fought in the Pacific against the Japanese. This was the new kind of sea war that revolved around aircraft carriers, bombers and fighter aircraft. The United States Navy did most of the fighting and won the important victories – for example, in the battles of the Coral Sea and Midway. The British Pacific Fleet – the 'forgotten fleet' – was dwarfed by the United States Navy and was able to play only a minor role. The final terror for those serving in the Far East was the kamikaze pilot. As a last, desperate ploy Japan sent more than 1200 planes on suicide missions to crash land on the aircraft carriers of the Pacific fleet. Every British carrier was hit, although none were sunk. Nevertheless, for the crews every kamikaze attack was a terrifying experience. Stuart Eadon was a junior officer on HMS *Indefatigable*, the first carrier to be hit in April 1945.

'I noticed an unidentified aircraft come round the bow of our ship and realized it was not one of ours. He was flying, I suppose, at just under 1000 feet, which is pretty low, and he banked. It all happened in a few seconds. As he banked I thumped the gunner on the back and shouted "Fire! fire! fire!" and the guns all blazed away and I could see our guns hitting the underbelly of the

Zeke. And within seconds the plane flashed over my head, about fifteen feet above, and I could clearly see this Jap pilot in green and yellow silks with his goggles on. And just a second later there was a terrific crump and his 500-pound [225-kilogram] bomb exploded. We lost fourteen killed that day… one of them was my cabin mate Len. I remember later I went back to my cabin and had a good cry. In years gone by we'd fought and fired against German Stuka dive bombers – but they always pulled out of the dive and you knew they were going to. But with the Jap, unless you stopped him he was going to come in and it always seemed he was coming straight for you.'

The D-Day landings on the beaches of Normandy, 6th June 1944. 17,000 Royal Marines took part in the action.

At the end of the war the Royal Navy emerged victorious, its proud traditions intact. Despite major losses in the early stages – the consequence of long neglect and deep conservatism – it had played a significant role in the victory. Its success ultimately owed much to the grit and determination of the ordinary seaman in the face of official incompetence. By the end of the war the Navy had expanded to an enormous size, with over 1000 warships and 3000 minor war vessels manned by 850,000 men. But the popular impression of invincible British sea power was largely illusory – the nation had been badly wounded by the conflict. She ended the war with huge debts and was faced by a clamour for independence in the Empire – beginning with India – which would result in a reduction in naval strength and a loss of her imperial navies and bases around the world. Perhaps most important, it had become clear during the course of the war that the United States – whose Pacific fleet dwarfed Britain's – had now established herself as the world's leading maritime power.

DAVID HOLMES

Born in Mitcham in Surrey, David was fifteen when he joined the Royal Navy in 1938. After training at HMS *Ganges* he joined his first ship, HMS *Barham*, as a gunner. In November 1941 he was on board when the *Barham* was torpedoed in the Mediterranean with the loss of hundreds of lives. After the war David served with the merchant navy until 1947, but, as a result of injuries sustained at sea, he came ashore and took a job with an engineering firm. He has been married three times and has been with his present wife for seventeen years. He has one son. David now lives in Maidenhead, Berkshire, where he spends his time writing and keeping in contact with old shipmates.

We feared nobody. Our motto was 'Always engage the enemy more closely' because we believed – and we knew – that we were the superior navy in the world. Nobody could touch us. And this is something that demands a man to live up to those standards and it's constantly drilled into you.

And I was drafted on to the battleship HMS *Barham*, which we believed was unsinkable. I was standing up forward on deck having a cup of tea. The first torpedo struck and I thought, phew, they're at us again, but it's nothing to

The sinking of HMS *Barham* by a U-boat on 24th November 1941. 861 officers and men, including the ship's captain, went down with her.

worry about. When the second one struck I thought, well, it may be something to be concerned about. And when the third and fourth struck I thought, now, there *is* something to be concerned about because you listed over at a terrific angle. But the rule is, if you leave the ship then you desert your ship in the face of the enemy. To be a survivor then the ship's got to leave you. You don't leave the ship, and that is something that is very strict and we're proud of in the Navy.

All of a sudden there was a big *whoof!*... an explosion, and she went up. Actually, it took four minutes from the first torpedo to the explosion, so it didn't give anybody much time to get off even if they wanted to. I went sailing in the air... but it's strange really what you think of in those circumstances. I was checking all my limbs to see if I'd got all my limbs before I hit the water. Once I hit the water the tidal wave from the explosion was coming into the sea and I was rolled over and over under the oily water. But I was fortunate 'cos I was a good swimmer and I swam until I came to an Australian ship called HMS *Nizam*. And all I can remember is an Australian saying 'Come on cobber, come up the scrambling net', and he helped me come on board and he took me down below and he laid me on the deck. As I lay there I felt what I thought was seaweed. I was brushing it to one side but when I looked it wasn't seaweed at all, it was the shipmate's intestines that had been blown out and his intestines were laying all over my hand. These sort of things you never forget.

We got in to the survivor's camp. It did rather shake you. I was terribly upset, good friends had been blown to smithereens and I used to dream about them a lot. But we had a job to do. The pride is still there. The Navy is still there and discipline is still there. We were the senior service and we were the silent service; therefore we didn't talk about it, we just got on with the job. It was my personal choice to join the Navy and I must take the consequences.

We were losing – I mean Malta itself was littered with sunken ships – but that made you even more determined that your ship would not be the next one. It got right into you. I still had this in my mind from childhood that I wanted to be the best gunner in the navy. And I was now aboard HMS *Kingston* and when I shot these planes down, I mean, I couldn't care less. To me they were enemy and that's it, I had to kill 'em. The more I killed the better. I wanted to rid the whole earth of these people. I was doing what I was paid to do and that was it. Bang, bang.

Then I changed after a young chappie died in my arms on board our ship. When you're cradling a man in your arms knowing full well his life is ebbing out of him and you can't do a thing about it, then you know what war's all about. Then came the pain, real pain of knowing what I was actually doing. Although in my subconscious that little voice was saying you want to be the best gunner in the navy, you want to be the best gunner in the navy, there was another voice saying, let's have compassion, show compassion. It's a very, very difficult situation to be in and when I shot the planes down I knew there was a different aspect there then. I was sorry for the people inside the plane. I didn't hate those men as individuals – I hated them for what they stood for.

When there's a lull in the action... now this is the worst time of all simply because you have more time to think about what you've done. How would I like that to happen to my brothers? – They're pilots. And its a terrible, terrible sensation; you actually start to realize what war is all about and what war means and what devastation, what heartbreak it causes and you think to yourself, well, what's it all for? But discipline always comes out on top. And our discipline said we were the best navy in the world. We were a proud people. We were a great nation. When we were at sea we realized that we had to win this war, it was a matter of pride. Britannia ruled the waves and that was a fact. And it would be unbearable if we had to surrender to another nation's navy.

CAPTAIN MERVYN WINGFIELD

Mervyn Wingfield joined the submarine branch in 1933 and by the outbreak of war, six years later, was in command of his own boat, HMS *Umpire*. The war finally gave him the chance to put into practice what he had trained for so long – 'to fire torpedoes which actually exploded'. In 1990 Mervyn returned to the Submarine Training School in Gosport, Hampshire, and presented them with the prized skull and crossbones ensign that he had flown so many times when captain.

My first command was in an H-class submarine. In my opinion these submarines were quite unfit for World War II – they were World War I submarines. They were very small and very primitive, very slow, much slower than the U-boats, and I didn't achieve any success at all. I had a try once after a long attack on a U-boat, which I eventually fired at. Unfortunately I made a mistake... it turned out to be a lighthouse on the Dutch coast and the lighthouse keeper must have been rather surprised to see two torpedoes explode at the foot of the lighthouse.

We had a lot of losses in those days and we were losing one or two a month and it was a bit depressing. There was always a knot of next-of-kin and relatives at the gates of the dockyard or barracks when we came into port; it was the relatives of some submarine that was overdue and had probably been lost.

But I don't think it lowered morale in the least – we expected losses in the war. I did several patrols on the Norwegian coast, most of them blank, but I did sink one ship – in fact it was the first one I sank. It was a medium-sized freighter going up the coast inside the islands and I managed to get in a position to fire and I fired, I think, four torpedoes and hit with two. And she was steaming along and slowly her bows went down and her stern cocked up and she steamed beneath the water with her propellers still turning. I was very pleased with that, my first success on that patrol. It was rather like hitting a perfect drive down the middle of the fairway or shooting a high pheasant. That was the only feelings I had, I regret to say. It may sound rather callous but they were all trying to kill us and so we had to kill them... as many as possible.

Fortunately, I was only a short time in the H-boats and then I got a newer submarine which unfortunately was sunk – sunk by one of our own side, an armed trawler that rammed me. He thought I was a U-boat and it's not very pleasant to talk about it because we lost most of the crew. I was picked up by

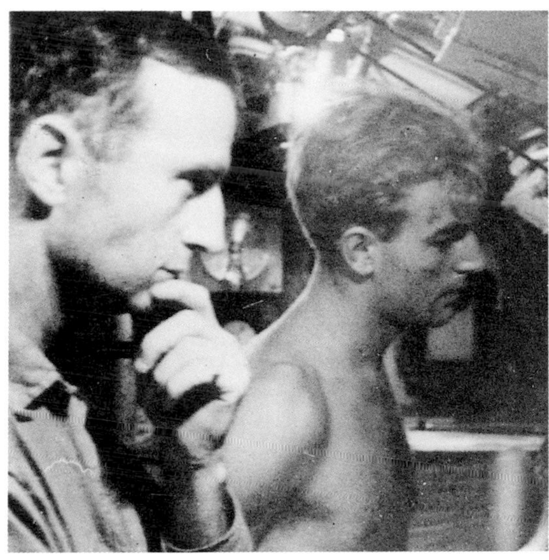

Captain Mervyn Wingfield (left) in action on the submarine *Taurus* in 1943.

the ship that sank us; they thought I was dead when they picked me up. I'd been rather a long time in the North Sea and the first thing I heard was one of them saying, 'Well, I'm afraid he's gone but we've got his name', and they were reading the bracelet with my name on it and I said 'I'm not dead. How many other survivors are there?', and they said 'Well you're the only one so far', and I said 'Well I think you'd better throw me back because I'm the captain – it doesn't do for the captain to be the sole survivor'. And they said 'No, we won't do that… have some rum'.

Later on I got another submarine called the *Sturgeon*, which was oldish but not as old as the H-boats, and there I had quite a successful time. I went to north Russia and operated under the Commander-in-Chief Northern Fleet. Later on I got an even newer submarine, the *Taurus*. I did two and a half years in her and we had even more successes. We were all fairly competitive and we kept our scores of sinkings. And we used to have a flag – we called it the Jolly Roger – which we flew on coming into the harbour after a patrol. That showed the ships you'd sunk and the gun actions you'd had.

One interesting operation I had was a battle with horse cavalry up in the north Aegean near the Bulgarian frontier. I think I'm right in saying that I'm the only submarine that had a battle with horse cavalry in World War II We were inside this harbour sinking all the ships, small kayaks and things, when there was a cloud of dust on the hillside and down the mountainside came a squadron of horse cavalry. They got on to the dockside and we were rather too close and they dismounted guns from the horses and started firing point-five machine guns at us. Well, I turned my bows to seaward and went off at full speed, but we did get a lot of hits. I was all right because I was behind the forward periscope – which was a thick one. And we had an Oerlikon gun, which we was firing back at the horse cavalry – never hit any of course. Then the chap firing this – the Oerlikon gunner – left his gun and came forward and said 'I've got to see the coxswain, I'm wounded'. And I said 'Well, not very badly wounded', and he said 'Oh, I've got a wound, I'm entitled to medical attention'.

And I said 'Well, we're in the middle of battle… you're not supposed to leave your gun in the middle of a battle'. And he said, 'I've got to see the coxswain'. So I said 'All right, go on then. Number one, would you take over the Oerlikon and fire it.' By that time we were getting fairly long range. So he sat down and pulled the trigger and put half a pan of Oerlikon into the first floor of the local hotel. The chap who was wounded – the crew gave him an awful bad time; they said, 'It's called cowardice in the face of the enemy. You left your gun and the Captain will court martial you and shoot you in the morning.'

So he had rather an unpleasant night. I operated on him first, on the ward-room table, to get this bullet out. I thought this was a good thing. We gave him a rum, then we had one ourselves, and I got an appropriate weapon out – which turned out to be a Gillette razor blade – and cut his foot open and got a pair of pointed pliers from the engine room and pulled out the bullet. This was all right and he made a good recovery. But he had a bad night because every time a sailor passed his bunk they said 'The Captain's going to shoot you in the morning', and in the morning the Coxswain said 'What do you think about this court martial?', and I said 'I think there might be a bit of trouble of we court martial him and condemn him to be shot'. The Coxswain said 'Yes, I think he's had a pretty bad time… how about we let him go?'. And so we let him go! I didn't see him again until I visited him in hospital and the doctor said, very curious wound, the bullet wound was quite normal but he couldn't understand all those cuts down his metatarsal bones. I said 'Well, that was where I was looking for the bullet with my razor blade'.

The most disagreeable experience of all was to be depth-charged, and we got depth-charged quite a lot. I always slowed down so as to be absolutely silent and altered course ninety degrees and, well, it usually worked. That's why I'm here! The noise is awful and you think you're going to be sunk any minute – that's part of the thing. You feel a jolt as if someone is giving the submarine a good shake. But when you're being depth-charged, as Captain, you had to be careful not to show that you were as frightened as you were, so I used to cross my legs to stop anybody seeing my knees knocking together. And then you had other manifestations of fear where you felt you wanted to have a pee all the time… and yet another one, you got frightfully thirsty. That was all right because my faithful steward would pass me a gin and tonic right in the middle of it – right in the middle of the depth-charging.

But gradually the depth charges faded away and we were okay to surface. And a funny thing happened once in the height of a depth-charging. We were somewhat damaged and we were sneaking away and then there were another six depth charges. And one of the ratings wrote something on a bit of paper which he handed to the coxswain – who smiled and handed it to me. And written on it was 'Request permission to revert to general service'... I read this out and everybody laughed. It released the tension.

SIDNEY GRAHAM

Sid was born in London's East End in 1920, the son of a seaman from Barbados. He dreamt of following in his father's footsteps and, at the age of 15, ran away to sea and became galley boy on the *Nernta*, a merchant ship sailing to South America. During the war he served on Atlantic and Arctic convoys as a merchant seaman. He married Esther in 1944 and they had thirteen children. Sid and Esther still live in the East End, not far from the dock where Sid would board the ships that took him around the world. He left the sea in 1960 but still meets up for a drink with his old seafaring mates. He and Esther look forward to visits from their 34 grandchildren and 15 great-grandchildren.

You was always on edge, know what I mean? You could never settle down. If you were sleeping you always got something on your mind – like torpedoes, I wonder if we're going to make the trip, things like that. But you knew what you had signed on for when you went on the ship.

Of course we were the lowest of the low, the stokers. They used to lock us in when an attack began. They used to come and lock what we called the 'fiddly door'... it used to go above your boilers to the top, come out on the companionway. If you got hit anywhere you had no chance of getting up the ladders over the boilers because your fiddly was locked. And if they hit them boilers, the boilers would go up and the whole ship breaks into half, *whoosh*, and that's it. Do you think it's easy? You're working your nuts off down there with them fires all the time... you think to yourself, Jesus, I wonder if we're going to make it or not. All sorts of silly things run through your head. You look and say, what would be the best way if you can escape? You're looking for the best way for yourself. Every man for himself, you know, but you've got no chance 'cos of the fiddly that's locked.

The night we got torpedoed I was up on the four-to-eight watch and I was talking to my friend Sid. Then he went down below and that's the last time I see

Sidney Graham pictured whilst he was serving on the Merchant convoys.

him. He got it in number one stokehole, wallop. And I was caught in the bathroom with a fellow named Chang. Tough, Chinese boy, born in Jamaica. I was having a bath and in them days we had to bathe in a bucket and when we got torpedoed I went up in the air and hit my ribs on the washbasin... busted 'em. Then the door slammed and this Chang was such a strong fellow he broke the door open. And as we were going out the men were running and one fellow he said, 'What's happened Sir?', and I said 'We've been tin-fished'.

Well, I got up on the companionway and walked along and that's when the submarine started to shell us. Wasn't going down quick enough for him. I was badly hit in the arm... I'll show you if you don't believe me, I had a big operation in the seaman's hospital, they thought they were going to lop me arm off. So I went in the lifeboat and we go away from the ship and the ship went down. And we could see her go and she started to explode... she went down, *whoof*, went down backwards.

Admiral Dönitz had apparently said 'Don't take no survivors – kill 'em, get rid of 'em'. He gave them that order, and you could hear the submarine chugging around trying to find us. Chug, chug, zoom – 'cos you hear – zoom, zoom, chug, chug. But they didn't find anybody. Luckily enough we were in the Caribbean, not in the cold, but we didn't know where we were going.

The officer on our lifeboat was the chief mate. He used to give us four ounces [about one-tenth of a litre] of water per day, that's all. Every morning he used to measure it out, and you used to drink it and they used to give you some hard biscuit with, like, Marmite on. We used to get one of them a day but oh, to eat it, it was murder. It's not the hunger, it's the thirst that gets hold of you, and the old chief mate used to tell us: 'Don't drink any of the salt water 'cos you'll never stop and you'll go and jump over the wall'. So we wouldn't touch the salt water.

There were sharks about, but being seamen we always called 'em 'nobbies' – that was a nickname for 'em, nobbies. They used to come and float around, come on at the boat, give you a look, rub their scales and try and knock it. And you'd make a noise and beat the sides of the boat with the oar – bang, bang,

bang – and they'd float away. They can't stand noise we was told, so that's what we done. Happily it worked.

We was nine days, getting on ten days, in the boat when we see an island. The officer said to us 'It'll either be Martinique or one of the other little islands... if it's Martinique they will intern us'. So we had a vote on the boat. Everybody had to vote. Everybody said 'We'll carry on, we'll take our chances', and that's what happened... we sailed into Barbados the next day. Didn't *sail* in – we waved to them and they towed us in the harbour. And when we got off the lifeboat you were walking funny, staggering all over the place because you was cramped up all the time and your limbs was finished. Then they put us in the seaman's mission, took us straight to the store, lined us up with coats, trousers and slippers, everything we needed, 'cos we lost everything. We had something to eat and went to bed, went to sleep.

But in those days as soon as you got torpedoed on them ships your money was stopped right away. That's the truth. Everybody kicked up a bit 'cos you couldn't walk about with nothing in your pockets, could you, let's be fair – and all the rum shops were open! Only thing they give us was our clothes... we couldn't walk about *naked*, could we. Well, we felt devastated because you didn't think they'd ever treat you like that. Because they treated you like you were an underrated citizen although you were doing your bit for your country, know what I mean? It's hard to think what you been through and what you were doing... and they treat you like that. They kidded us you'll have a better life and all that. What did we get? Didn't get no life, did we. I even had to fight for me pension, me state pension.

COMMANDER RONNIE HAY

He is everybody's ideal image of the dashing wing commander and enjoys talking about what he calls his 'antics and exploits'. Born in 1916, Ronnie joined the Fleet Air Arm in 1938 to train as a pilot. Although he was involved in many vicious air battles during the war he remained devoted to naval aviation, which he regarded as a crucial arm of the service. Ronnie married Barbara, a Wren, in 1944 and they had four children. After he retired in 1966 he spent his time chartering yachts around Europe and in the Mediterranean. He lives with Barbara in their secluded, rambling home in Wiltshire.

The aeroplanes I flew in the early days were the Gladiator, which was a very nice little aeroplane but the sort of toy you'd like to have in your back garden, not really to fight a war with. And the other was the Blackburn Skua – and such an abortion of an aircraft has not been seen for a long while! Of course, there were other ones that were even worse than that, like the Shark. These were all quite horrible aeroplanes – very slow, underpowered – but they did actually land and take off from carriers and we could carry a bomb. And they had four machine guns firing forwards, so at least you had some air defence. We had an old Lewis gun from World War II in the back cockpit that the rear gunner could use. We did in fact sink the first cruiser in history from a Skua in one of the fjords in Norway, so it wasn't impossible – but it was very vulnerable, very slow and ill-armed.

If you encountered any aircraft of the German Air Force, unless he was flying towards you the chances of you catching him up was nil, so you had to have some sort of slight height advantage and dive down on them. When you heard the news that there were bandits or large enemy formations approaching it was not a very pleasant sensation. But you had to get up off the carrier and get it over with and you climbed as high as you could to get above the chaps. And you often saw this vast armada beneath you and it was like a mouse looking at a huge cheese... where does he start nibbling? So we'd dive in.

Commander Ronnie Hay in 1943 when he was a Squadron Commander in the Fleet Air Arm – 'the Lord God Almighty of aviators'.

But in some ways we were safer upstairs than they were downstairs. I remember being bombed by the Italians in the Mediterranean ... a great Italian armada came over the fleet and we were shooting a few of them down on the way. But something like eighty of them would come and drop their bombs and the entire British fleet would disappear in a fury of smoke and you simply couldn't see the fleet at all and you wondered where you were going to spend the night.

That was a worry sometimes, not knowing where the carrier was. If you didn't have much fuel you'd perhaps only have twenty minutes flying time left to look for her before you had to land in the sea – and if you landed in the sea that would be the end of you. Because sometimes the ship was not where it was meant to be. Then of course they did have this beacon, which did help you to home in on the ship, but there was no radio communication. So when the beacon didn't work and visibility was not very good, lots of cloud about, it all added to the stress.

It all changed about 1942. The differences between the American equipment that we got – the Hellcats and the Corsairs and the Avengers – with what we had before… it totally changed the war. We did not have our hands tied behind our back like we did in the old days – it was like heaven on earth you might say. We were able to dictate the terms to the enemy then.

But no one enjoys killing and risking being killed and I think we were overflown. It really started to tell towards the end of the war. If they'd seen their friends shot down in flames into the sea or had a bad accident landing on deck some of the men would be visibly shaking all over. The flight commander would say, 'Come on, pull yourself together', and give him a snort. If he was sent to me… I was the Squadron Commander, I was the Lord God Almighty for aviators in those days… the chap would be quaking with fear – nothing to do with the combat outside! 'Now sonny,' I'd say, 'look, relax, I'm going to buy you a drink', and we drank it, and I said 'You'll be as right as rain in the morning, we've all been through this, we've all lost friends'. That was how we dealt with it, and alcohol helped a lot.

We all got a sort of twitch. I nearly passed out once in the air with noise. In fact I'm half deaf now – singing in the ears, noise of the engines – all that's going on. If you wanted to be relieved of the job they called it LMF, which is 'lack of moral fibre'. It was a bloody insult to those poor aviators who had got the twitch so badly they just flew into the sea and killed themselves. There's no doubt that at the end there were a number of people for whom the war couldn't end quickly enough. I may say I was one of them.

STAN BLACKER

Stan was born in Shepton Mallet, Somerset, in 1924, the son of a railway porter. At 14 he began work as an apprentice in the building trade. He joined the Royal Marines in 1941. The defining moment of his own service came on D-Day in 1944, when Stan was one of thousands of Allied troops who took part in the assault on the Normandy coast. He has been married to Kathleen for 52

years and they have two sons. His mischievous sense of humour and warmth have made Stan a popular figure in Shepton Mallet and he now spends much of his time involved in the local Royal Marines Association. He still insists, however, that he is no hero.

We trained at Lympstone and did six weeks square-bashing and ended up at Dulwich. And the conditions there were so bad it was reported that people committed suicide there. Training was hard and you were continuously driven. They issued orders that too many youngsters were being killed at 18 so they wouldn't send them overseas until 19.

Well, in the build up to D-Day every youngster was collared. They put us through five camp trainings and finally our landing-craft training. But we had no faith in our craft – they were old and unreliable and we were told that it would take a quarter million lives to breach the Atlantic wall. They duplicated each crew for every craft and we knew then that we were expendable. Our craft didn't inspire much confidence – it was the smallest vessel used, 50 feet [15 metres] in length, two tons and a completely open deck. It was powered by two nine-horsepower engines which did nine knots flat out and we had to cross 90 miles [145 kilometres] of Channel. We were then issued with 60 rounds of ammunition for our rifles and stripped of all our identity bar two bakelite discs showing our name, number and religion. Apparently it doesn't matter how much your body is blown to bits, the discs stay intact.

We were told we'd be sailing on 4th June, but that was cancelled due to stormy weather. The next day Lieutenant Jimmy Ball gathered us together and all the flotillas knelt in three rows all the length of the camp road. Out came the vicar and said a short prayer: 'God give you courage to face the enemy' – and if we could have run away we would. During those final weeks all our letters were censored and we had to make a will. None of us had anything to leave 'cos we were on two bob [ten pence] a day, but the officer said if you don't make a will you'll be on a charge. We thought as we sailed down the River Hamble we was sailing to our death.

It was a bad, bad day; the sea was running high and 'twas black and overcast. We had a tough job to make our way out through the boom defence in Portsmouth harbour and as we sailed on a merchant ship signalled to us 'minefield ahead'. There were green flags on buoys in the water. No nobody told us about green flags, and if that merchant ship had not signalled we'd have sailed straight into the minefield.

We could see all the French coast on fire. Imagine the chaos – there was our fleet firing into Normandy, the Germans firing back, there was ships being sunk. The beach was jam-packed with vehicles, troops the beachmasters were fighting hard to sort out into some sort of formation. Eventually we got into the beach and unloaded, and away again to ferry more stuff in, but there were tanks that had gone down in the soft sand, right down, with just part of their turrets showing, there was troops floating face down in the water what had been killed, there were craft smashed to pieces on the beach and there was all the obstacles which we were later to see under the water – which was sharp pieces of iron to rip the bottoms off the boats. Another hazard the Germans had planted was logs with bombs that floated up and down on chains which were anchored. We were constantly showered with bullets from the German defences whilst working.

At nightfall we had to put to sea and canisters of smoke was released from the ships that covered the whole fleet. The next day, because there were very few of our flotilla left, it was decided to hold a meeting on the beach and suddenly a German fighter appeared and he came on and on and on and nothing fired at it and he dropped this bomb and killed my commanding officer and about six others about forty yards from us. Everything started firing, but to my knowledge he got away.

And as we stood there – we'd been blasted with sand and everything – and Merrick came running up the beach and he said 'Captain Gooding, our commanding officer's killed', and he were crying like a baby 'cos he had great affection for his commanding officer. We were sorry to have lost him, but we were jubilant that we'd made it and we'd landed and the stuff had gone ten miles [16 kilometres] in on the first day. The resistance was nothing like anticipated and we continued ferrying them for several months, and would put to sea when it was foggy. You never seen such a concentration of stuff and that's what few people realize – that it was the biggest invasion ever seen or organized in the world.

Stan Blacker in his dress uniform in 1944. D-Day proved the greatest for Stan and thousands of other Royal Marines.

5

Women Who Dared

There was a powerful taboo against women working at sea during the first half of the century. The assumption that only men could cope with the danger and hard physical labour involved in a life at sea was strongest in the Royal Navy, on merchant cargo ships and in the fishing industry. It was unimaginable, too, that a woman should be allowed to join a lifeboat crew. This was a man's world, and in an era when it was generally believed that women were the weaker sex whose natural place was in the home, this rigid division of labour was largely unquestioned. Although a few women worked on passenger liners or went to sea as the captain's wife, there was fierce resistance to the idea that the sea was a proper place for a woman to be. Most sailors hated having women on board as they felt that they had to control their language and behaviour. There were also a host of superstitions – especially prevalent in fishing communities – that revolved around the idea that a woman on a boat was likely to bring ill fortune and disaster to the rest of the crew. This weight of male tradition and prejudice ensured that very few women did go to sea – but the lives of those who did are all the more remarkable for it.

It is surprising how many of these women were from a well-to-do background. The sea offered an escape from the narrow confines of gentility and domesticity for the most independent and adventurous young women of the

Hull fisherwomen in the 1940s. It was extremely rare for a woman to go out in a fishing boat – they were thought to bring bad luck.

time. The only British woman to become a ship's engineer, Victoria Drummond, was the god-daughter of Queen Victoria. Her father used his influence in shipping companies to overcome the resistance to the idea of a woman following this career in the 1920s. Dorothy Laird, the daughter of an architect, used the money she had saved as a writer of romantic fiction to pay to be a deck hand on one of the last of the commercial sailing ships, the *Penang*, in the 1930s. She was not the only young woman working on the sailing ships that made the dangerous journey around Cape Horn. A small coterie of like-minded, bohemian, middle-class women were climbing aloft to unfurl the sails, often attracted by the freedom and beauty of life at sea.

Most middle-class women who went to sea in the pre-war years were captain's wives. They had long enjoyed the privilege of being the sole woman on board a cargo-carrying merchant ship. In the days of sailing ships they had to be a tough breed. Some would nurse injured crew members, help with the cooking or encourage the men when faced with danger. Others learned navigational skills from their husbands. There were a few celebrated cases of captain's wives

Left: **Holidaymakers return from a shrimping expedition in 1934. The only opportunity most women had to go fishing was on pleasure trips like these.**

Below: **Making fishing nets in Grimsby in 1931. Women played an important role in the fishing industry but it was not restricted to work ashore.**

taking over the ship altogether. In the 1920s Mrs Patten, whose husband commanded the clipper *Neptune's Car*, took command off Cape Horn when her husband went blind. The mate had previously been arrested for insubordination and the second mate could not navigate, so Mrs Patten, then only 24, successfully took the ship from the Horn to San Francisco, a journey of 52 days. For the most part, however, especially in the age of steam and diesel, the captain's wife had a more leisurely role. Life could be a pleasurable round of dining, drinks, sunbathing and swimming – as it was for Sheila Henney, married to the captain of a BP oil tanker. All the domestic chores were done by servants and there were shopping and sightseeing to look forward to in every port of call.

Some women pursued their interest in the sea through yachting. A few had raced since Victorian times – one of the most celebrated was Miss Lord, helmswoman on the *Sea Belle*, a 92-foot schooner, who was quoted in *Yachting World* in 1884 as saying 'No man likes to be beaten by a woman'. But she was very much the exception. Most were barred from membership of yachting clubs before the First World War. These exclusive social clubs were decidedly upper class and male – the women were not expected to sail and certainly not to race, but rather to grace parties and attend the annual ball. The vast majority of women who flocked to Cowes in the Isle of Wight every year as part of the aristocratic 'season' played a similar role. These restrictions were gradually lifted during the inter-war years when the clubs were colonized by the middle class and most sailing and yachting clubs began to accept women members.

In fishing communities the traditional division of labour was that the women worked ashore, mending nets, gutting and selling fish, but work at sea was reserved for the men. It was extraordinarily rare for a woman to go out in a fishing boat – if it happened it would normally be the wife or daughter of the owner–skipper of a small boat, standing in because of illness or a severe shortage of hands. Dorothy Stephenson, brought up in the deep-sea fishing community of Hessle Road, Hull, in the 1930s remembers the fierce resistance to her ambition to work on the trawlers. She eventually managed to fulfil her dream of going to sea – but as a cook on a cargo ship.

Although very few British women fished in boats it was very different in some other countries – women crewed fishing boats, for example, in the Baltic coastal communities of Sweden, in southern Brittany and in northwest Spain. One of the few places in Britain where women did enter the exclusively male

Boat's Crew Wrens in action during the Second World War. The labour shortage in the Royal Navy gave women the opportunity to serve on boats for the first time.

world of work at sea was the Shetland Islands. Here, from the 1900s onwards, a few fishing boats were owned by women and registered in their names. Generally, however, the rigid division of labour between the sexes continued after the Second World War – although in an age when women were demanding greater freedom and equality some independent-minded women defied tradition to go to sea and earn their master's ticket. One of them was Liz Duvill, the daughter of a lobster fisherman on the northwest coast of Scotland.

Boat's Crew Wrens quickly came to be seen as the élite of the service.

In the Royal Navy there was a formal bar on women going to sea – the idea of women being involved in a war at sea was particularly shocking. However, in the Second World War the labour shortage on the home front provided the stimulus for what was seen at the time as an extraordinary experiment – training Wrens to handle boats and operate them in ports and harbours. It was all the idea of Mrs Welby, Superintendent of the Women's Royal Naval Service (WRNS – hence 'Wrens') in Plymouth, and it was put into practice in 1941 with the grudging acceptance of the Admiralty. The normal duties of the WRNS were clerical or domestic, so this was a venture into unknown territory. One hundred and sixty 'Boat's Crew Wrens' were recruited and trained in Plymouth. They quickly came to be seen as the élite of the service and proved such a success that Wrens were used in many other ports. Being one of those first women's boat crews is remembered as an exciting challenge, but it could be difficult and dangerous. Among their duties were dragging decomposing bodies from the water, driving boats through dark, mine-infested waters, firing Lewis guns at bombers overhead and escorting prisoners of war ashore. To begin with they often faced derision and discrimination from the men they served alongside. It was only by being as tough as the men that the women eventually won acceptance. Barbara Lorentzen used the skills she learned in the WRNS to become a skipper on a pleasure boat in Falmouth, Cornwall, just after the war.

The job a woman was most likely to get at sea was on a passenger ship. The big shipping lines like Cunard had long employed women as maids to tend to the needs of rich passengers or as nannies to look after the young children on board. From the 1920s women were recruited to do a range of other jobs on the big luxury liners: they worked, for example, as stewardesses, shop assistants, hairdressers, nurses, Turkish bath attendants, assistant pursers and telephonists. Although the women were often subject to strict and sometimes petty rules that reduced opportunities for social mixing with male passengers and staff, life on a luxury liner offered them a rare opportunity to travel and see the world. After the war passenger liners began to recruit more and more women to work in territory which had traditionally been male. But life on board was often difficult – as remembered by Betty Wood, who worked on emigrant ships between England and Australia in the late 1940s.

'When you signed on you were signed on as a seaman. You were a merchant seaman – and the photograph of you made you almost look like one! We looked quite nice in our uniform and we were quite young and presentable, but to most of the men you were an object to be pursued. It took a long time for them to accept that you were actually doing a job out there. They looked at you suspiciously, as though there were some ulterior motive. The fact that you wanted to go to sea for the joy of it... no one could understand that, that was beyond their comprehension.'

In the past few decades there have been more opportunities for women to go to sea than ever before. Since the war most yachting clubs have opened their doors to women members. In the late 1960s the Royal National Lifeboat Institution (RNLI) began to accept women as volunteers on lifeboats, and mixed crews are now common. In the 1990s women were enrolled as crew members on Royal Navy warships. Nevertheless, despite greater freedom and equality, the sea is still dominated by men and the assumption remains that a ship is not a proper place for a woman to work.

DOROTHY LAIRD

Dorothy was born in 1912 in Renfrewshire, Scotland. The daughter of an architect father and an artist mother, she was drawn to the beauty of sailing ships as a young journalist in 1934 when she made a voyage on the *Penang*. During the war she worked for the merchant navy and in Royal Navy Intelligence. She married John in 1945 and has since had a very successful career as an author, publishing almost forty books on various subjects. Widowed in 1995, Dorothy lives in Newmarket, Suffolk, and likes nothing better than watching the horses being put through their paces at the nearby racetrack. She has a son and a daughter. Taking pride of place in her small living room is a huge, detailed model of the *Penang*, made for her by one of the seamen with whom she sailed.

I was a young journalist and I wanted to record the sailing ships, which were disappearing. I wanted to document them. It was a whole world to explore. I was reading everything to try and learn as much as I could about the ships. And then I had to find one. I wanted a ship with royals and an open wheel – to get the beautiful views from the wheel – and, of course, a Master of good repute.

I'd got everything clued up, my parents approved of the Master, and then a letter came in from Finland – would I sign over a shilling stamp 'to pay for recovery of corpse'! That scuppered the whole thing. It was a very long process getting permission. However, Gustave Ericsson, who was nicknamed 'Great

Economy', hated to turn down good money and he was willing to put up with having females on his ships if they paid for the privilege, and I went on a fine four-masted barque to Finland.

When I came back I met another girl, Kat, who was mad keen and determined to go. The mate, a splendid seaman, tried to leave when he found there were women on board. The usual thing was said about being unlucky, but it was more that it was a macho thing – you were crowding in on their place.

Dorothy Laird takes the wheel of the *Penang* in 1934. Her passion for sailing ships has remained throughout her life.

In the *Penang* we sailed from Leith, in Scotland. This was our first big voyage. We sailed on the same tide as two other ships and we beat them both. It took us a couple of weeks to get clear of the channel. We were very tired. Every time you stopped you slept, ate a meal – anywhere. You worked Scandinavian hours, which were ten hours on one day and fourteen hours on the next. We were absolutely exhausted.

It was very hard work. I chipped acres of rust, red-leaded and painted and did a little bit of hauling. Eventually your hands hardened, but they were bleeding all over the place. You had cracks ... a filthy kind of fish oil was put on the wires to preserve them and it doesn't do any good to your hands.

When you were off the Horn you were soaking wet for about three weeks without any chance of getting dry. You've open cracks on your legs. You used to lay your socks along your thigh to get a little bit dry during the night. You got terribly dirty, too. We got each day a tin jug – that was our fresh water for the day – and we used to wash. And by the end the water would be solid.

As regards toilets, I was allowed to use the mates' loo. Occasionally in good weather the Master would let us have his bathroom for an 'all over'. The boys used to laugh when we were chipping the rust in the places they'd been using as loos.

Now hauling – I did a bit of that. Now a lot of these simple tasks are a damn sight more difficult than they look. By the way, you call nothing 'a rope'. They've all got different names. They either pull the yards up or they pull the sails down and so forth and they're known by that name. When you're on a brace and you've got a line of boys it'll be in order of merit – the good ones would be further up, you see. And then you have the hauling calls. Now, they are distinctive to each person and it had splendid rhythm – 'Hey Ho Yah! Ah Ho Yah!' – you knew from it who was hauling. Some hauling calls were made up entirely with swear words! You were in your own circle of sea and completely dependent on the people on board.

I used to go aloft. It was dangerous but I asked permission. Not to work, but to carry the sailmaker's bucket. He was an Australian Aborigine – a pearl diver – and he used to tell me all sorts of stories about his life, sitting upward of the gallant yard. It was absolutely wonderful. The ship is so beautiful and she's a narrow little thing and you're looking right down her and she's a wedge in the sea.

Of course a ship speaks you know, with all the sounds of the sea which are melting into each other. In good weather you get very little sound from the sea but the noise is mostly ship's noises. In the very bad weather I never went up, and I never went up at nights. If the Master said 'Don't go up', you didn't; you just obeyed the Master.

The most exhilarating time is going round the Cape – those huge seas are magnificent! You'd get down into a trough and see nothing, just the sea around you, and then gradually you lift up on this and go right up. The sea is between you and the light – at the very top of the sea is brilliant, emerald green. The sea itself is a menacing purply black. You get right up the top, then *whoosh!* – you go down the other side like skiing.

Water is the strongest thing you ever met. The west coast of New Zealand is sheer so you have no warning of coming up to it, so we had to heave to. When we were going under way again and turned head on she just shipped water. The whole length of her – hundreds of tons of water. My friend Kat wasn't a strong person... she was washed down, a little yellow blob going backwards and forwards across the ship. I thought I'd stop her, and of course down I went. So there were two blobs going back and front and the boys swearing like hell. Then it started draining off and the Mate jumped forward. They all looked absolutely thunder and said 'Up the poop women who can't keep their feet'.

I went down below and I fainted. When I came to I had a hole about the length of my sea boot and the bone had been slived off. I was in my bunk for three weeks after that.

Once we lost the main mast coming home from Australia. There's a big difference in a ship according to whether she carries cargo or not – it's a totally different movement. Coming out of the Tasman Sea you wait until you get a good strong wind. A west wind you go towards the Horn, an east wind you go towards the Cape. We went towards the Horn and suddenly one night we were hit by a very hard squall and she began to get wallopy. I got up and *poof!*... we went over on the side. Our port went under water and I didn't hear anything for the crash of dishes. The spanker had fallen. Complete silence – half the ship was under water. The Master sent us all below. We weren't moving, just lying on our side. The Captain was sitting there with a towel under his soaking wet arm and he had dividers and was working out the way the strain could be taken and transferred to the ship herself. There was no running, no shouting. I was stiff with nerves. The cook, a young lad, had obviously not slept. We had new loaves of bread, coffee and tea and everyone was silent and you didn't hear a single person swear for three days – and then it sounded lovely!

Well, afterwards the third mate said it would be 'roll, roll, roll' all the way to New Zealand. We were desperate to save the ship and nothing was cut away, everything was saved. In fact the boys took tremendous risks trying to get hold of the wreckage that was over the side. People worked so hard. I wanted to go on my watch in the morning but the Mate refused because it was too dangerous, so my part in the great adventure was to polish brass and wash dishes, but you did it very willingly because you were being accepted by them. You see, you were closer to the people at that time than with anyone else in your life.

It was a wonderful time at sea and, you see, you use the winds. I mean, they're named... and the most beautiful wind is probably the Southeast Trade, which is absolutely beautiful – sparkling, lovely stars at night and lots of flying fish and absolutely gorgeous. The biggest and strongest winds are in the southern hemisphere, and there you have very little land and therefore the seas and the winds get up and up and up and there's nothing to stop them or slow them down. You are ruled by the wind and you are learning of them all the time and the seamen are learning and you are in touch with the Cooks and the Darwins. You felt exalted – it was something that was exhilarating beyond all belief.

It changed you completely. Sometimes I get the same feeling when I meet some seamen that we're in tune with – a simplified, not particularly intelligent, but simplified and understandable way of life. You get to know what is important and what is not. Somehow you discard a lot of things. You're not frightened... you might be frightened of dying but you're not frightened of death. And, gradually, as a woman you became accepted as one of them and sometimes when we went to visit other ships when you came into port they enjoyed showing you off a little bit and if someone asked them something instead of answering they said 'Dorothy'll tell you that'... they enjoyed showing you off.

DOROTHY STEPHENSON

Dorothy welcomes you to her home like an old friend. She shares her modest bungalow in Gloucestershire with her many dogs, who clearly adore her. A well-known and respected breeder of champion show dogs, Dorothy's earlier life could not be further removed. She was born in 1929, the only daughter of a trawler skipper, and can clearly remember the path that took her from the tough Hessle Road fishing community of Hull to a life at sea as a ship's cook in the post-war years. Dorothy wouldn't say how many times she had been married, only that she was nineteen the first time and there have been 'several' since. She has two daughters and a son. Funny and fiercely independent, she now prefers to live wholly without men, who, she says, 'never knew how to deal with me'.

The first thing I remember was Dad telling stories to me mum at the table when he used to come back from sea. All the places that he used to go to, it was romantic. He used to talk about going to 'Bear Island'. Now, to a kid, the first thing you'd think of is it's full of bears. 'Oh, I'm going to Greenland'... well, to me it was all green and you imagined mountains and rivers. 'I'm going to Iceland'... that's all ice and you think of icebergs and polar bears and penguins. And this is what first started me off wanting to go to sea.

We used to go down and collect Dad's wages and the first thing you're told as a girl is 'Don't go on a ship'. Now the boys could run on the ships, but the girls couldn't, they were kept back. Many a time when I was a bairn I wanted to run to me father and me mother'd hold me back – no, I wasn't allowed near the boats. And it used to get right up my nose because even when I was little I wanted to go on ships. Of course, then as you get older you learn that the superstition is that women are not allowed on board ship, its unlucky. It's very, very unlucky. I mean if a ship didn't land any fish and a woman had stood on it it was her fault!

Really I was a fisherman in a woman's body. All through our family, right the way down for generations there'd been fishermen and I didn't see why I couldn't go. Course, every time I said I wanted to go to my father... well, I won't tell you his comment. He said no in no uncertain terms. 'Why not?' I'd say. 'Because you're not a lad.' And I was unhappy because I loved the sea. It's as though when you're born from a fisherman or a seaman half of your blood is

Dorothy Stephenson pictured with her younger brother in the late 1930s. Dorothy refused to accept the commonly held belief that women should not go to sea, and later worked on a merchant ship.

salt water... it's just an automatic steering system you've got.

But it didn't put me off. So when I was at school I used to play 'twag' – that was our term in Hull for not going when you should be going. Me mother used to have pennies on the mantelpiece and I used to take some and go down to the ferry. And I used to stay there all day... backwards and forwards from Hull to Lincoln. I just used to watch the river, I was so happy.

When I first left school... my granny was a herring woman from Peterhead and she got me a job in Tethers – she was a forewoman there. My first job was underneath a herring-gutting machine, catching the melts as they came out the matching. It stunk. Then I learnt to split. You're doing the same thing all day, but you can dream and all I dreamt of was going to sea. Then I moved to another place on the fish dock, and this one was so close to the dockside you were right by the ships. And when we used to finish work there was two or three of us used to go on the ship. Course, it was late, and all that was on it was a watchman. We used to pretend to be running the ship, and I'd get in the wheelhouse and I'd be the skipper. Didn't know a thing about it, but I used to pretend. You lived in cloud-cuckoo-land and we used to run up and down the deck and pretend we was hauling in the nets. We'd imagine we was at Bear Island and I'd be looking out for the whales... and the watchman used to come and chase us off – 'Bad luck, get off, you've no right on 'ere' – and we used to run like hell, you know, and that was a normal thing.

But it was a dream, you was dreaming, and I mean I wasn't the only girl. There was lots of lasses used to want to go to sea, but it was a no-no. As soon as you asked you were cut off, dead; there was no chance. Some of them lost that feeling, some of them married fishermen, went their own way – but with me I never lost it.

I got married and I had my kids; I got them off my hands, done me duty – that was it as far as I was concerned. And I was going out with this German fella, Manfred, he was an engineer on a German cargo ship called the *Vidor*. One day he said 'We've lost the bloody cook, he just walked off and left us'. So I don't know why, but all of a sudden I just went dry from the top of me hair to me feet and I said, 'Will *I* do?... *I'll* come'. 'Oh,' he said, 'you'd save our life.' I said, 'Only for a fortnight'. And I stayed three year. Loved every minute of it.

Well, when I stepped on the ship, stand on the wood for the first time, *plonk, plonk*, I thought, I've arrived. The exhilaration! I thought all my birthdays had come at once. The cook was normally a man – he used to sleep with the men. I couldn't do that, so the skipper said I could take the first-aid room. German ships had a different attitude to women in those days – you were not regarded as a women *per se*, you were regarded as a member of the crew. And as we sailed out of the Humber we was in the North Sea. I took me pan of spuds and all me veg and I sat astern on the ship and I was just looking out. I was peeling potatoes but I never looked at one – I wasted more than I did. I could smell it... I was there... I was happy!

It was hard graft being the cook, but I didn't mind. The only thing that used to frighten me when I was at work was if it was bad weather. All of a sudden the ship would go up at one end and down at the other and you risked getting scalded... getting burnt with the fat as things spilled off the stove. The next thing you had not flying saucers but flying plates; it was nothing to have a cabbage crack you on the back of the head. You'd have to duck. Things would come at you like missiles because things weren't battened down.

Whenever I could I used to go up and help the crew. That wasn't my job but I liked to do it. I used to go and help 'em tie all the timbers down. I used to have more fun doing that than anything else. Until one day I got blown overboard. But luckily I was tied up... they used to tie a rope around me. The rope was heavier than me, I didn't weigh ten stone [63.5 kilograms]. The ship listed to port and the next thing I knew I'm hanging over the side and I'm in the water, freezing cold. I mean three minutes in there and you're dead duck. I'm screaming my head off. They dragged me back and I'm shivering like a little dog shitting razor blades. Put me near the galley and they're rubbing me off, ripping me clothes off, and I'm saying 'Having a good time?!' – and they said 'Yes, but we've got to keep you warm!'.

Me and Manfred we got very close – we were lovers, pure and simple. Any woman that goes to sea and says she's never had an affair, she's a liar, and I don't care what woman it is and I don't care what position she holds. You're in a closed community, you always pick somebody up you like or they pick you up. You're so close and the things that happen make you closer. It was a very happy relationship. I shared his cabin sometimes and sometimes he shared mine. We wanted to get married at one time and then I went off the idea. I get bored very easily with men. If they haven't got an intellect I don't want to know 'em. He was a gentleman but he didn't have any real intellect. He didn't stimulate me. I've always wanted to learn – learn about different cultures.

What I loved most of all about going to sea was that everything was different, the people were different, it was just like a new world to me. I could imagine Christopher Columbus sailing to America, finding the Incas and saying 'God, it's different to where I come from!'. It is. You can understand why they wanted the adventure. That's what I wanted. I wanted to conquer new worlds, I wanted to see everything different. We used to go to Frankfurt... went to the opera house there. Never in my life did I imagine anything could be so beautiful. And that was where I got a little bit of culture. I heard my first opera, Aida... fell in love with it. I've been a fanatic ever since. I didn't know what opera was 'til I went to sea.

It seemed like the world is a like a big patchwork quilt in 3-D and every country you go to is different. When you go to different cities something always strikes you as different. When we went up the Rhine you'd see all the different German houses on the side and you'd see storks on top of the chimneys. I'd never seen a stork in my life. And going up the Rhine you'd see deer running down to the water's edge. It fascinated me.

Anyway, after three years I wasn't homesick, but I wanted to see me mum, I wanted to get back to me bairns, so I came back to Hull. But out of those years at sea I got a great self-satisfaction. I learned a lot, I saw things I would never have seen if I hadn't done it. I'd had dreams of making an epic journey and I made that epic journey and I did it on my own.

SHEILA HENNEY

Sheila travelled over one million miles to sea with her husband, the captain of a BP oil tanker, and still goes on a cruise once a year. 'I've had the most fabulous life', she says. Sheila was born in Grantham, Lincolnshire, where her father was a doctor, in 1912. She studied languages at London University before meeting her husband in 1934 and embarking on what she calls her 'life of

luxury' as the only woman on board her husband's ship. Now widowed, Sheila remains a strong-willed and outspoken woman. Although she finds walking difficult, she still likes to go shopping and even has a chauffeur who takes her from her home town of Bexhill in East Sussex to visit friends and relatives.

My love of the sea started as a little girl and I can remember learning to swim when I was about six years old. I used to swim with my grandfather, who lived by the sea, and I used to jump off a very high diving board astride a rubber horse and I used to disappear beneath the waves and come back up still astride the rubber horse. Yes, I adored the sea. When I was very young we went to Holyhead to go across to Ireland on holiday and I could smell the tarred ropes. It was thrilling. And then when I heard Welsh sailors talking to each other in a language which I couldn't understand I was absolutely thrilled. When we sailed I thought the sea was an extraordinarily interesting piece of nature, and from there that is how I got my love of the sea. In those days girls didn't go to sea, but I decided I would like to go to sea for my life.

My whole family were doctors and they wanted me to follow that line. My father took it for granted that I also would be a doctor. Well, I told him that if he'd ever listened to me, from the age of nine I've wanted to go to sea. I think he made a little, slightly sarcastic laugh and the matter was closed. I ended up with a degree in languages. Then I took up domestic science. I thought, I'm going to get married and that'll be handy.

I met a lot of students and made quite good friends, and one night a party of eight of us were going to go to a big charity dance at the Waldorf Hotel, up in London. Anyway, I met a very nice man and I said, 'What are you studying?'. He said 'I'm studying for my ticket'. Well, I hadn't a clue what a 'ticket' was. So I said, 'Oh, what's that for?'. 'Well,' he said, 'I'm a seafarer... I'm taking my final exams, eventually to become Master of a ship.' Well, I decided whilst we were dancing that I'd get to know him well during the months he was in London, get to know his family, and I was going to marry him. I liked him immensely straight away and I decided then that I would have my life at sea, and I did.

In 1945, as soon as the war was over, I joined him and started the life I'd always planned for myself. Except that I didn't have a job to do – I was a passenger. We had beautiful, beautiful accommodation. We had our own private sitting room, bedroom and bathroom and we had an Indian steward who worked for us. The only thing I let him do was my white shoes and one or two little things like that and he did all my husband's laundry, but I did my own.

Sheila Henney pictured during one of her many voyages on her husband's oil tanker in the 1950s.

The Indian crews were very, very respectful. When my Indian servant came into my cabin he would remove his sandals outside and come in bare-footed, which was very respectful. You had to be careful when you were changing and dressing.

Sometimes when we went ashore he would be waiting on our return. It didn't matter whether it was midnight or two in the morning, he'd be sitting cross-legged and bare-footed outside our accommodation, waiting to see if there was anything needed. Also, if we had Indian crews we'd have an awful lot of Indian food. I couldn't stand Indian food before I got to sea with the Indians, but afterwards I thought it was wonderful. They used to do all the genuine preparations – chop and hammer and bang and bash and in the end you'd get delicious meals.

Sometimes I used to take one or two of the Indians ashore with me when they were off duty and they would carry big baskets on their heads. When I went shopping I just sort of threw things at them and they put them into the baskets. On one occasion I bought a large carpet – which was rolled up and the two of them carried it through all those crowded alleyways and streets and they never showed any disgruntlement on their faces.

My day was so pleasurable. Our Indian servant brought us tea and breakfast and then I would get up and have my shower and go along to the swimming pool and have my swim. If the weather was very hot I would stay in quite a time. The water was very warm and occasionally an officer would come with a bucket of cold water, ice water, and tip it over me and I had lots of fun. Afterwards I'd go and have coffee with someone. It might be the Chief Engineer. Then I'd go back to my cabin, shower and try and do something with my hair, get dressed, and we always had drinks then with the senior officers.

I used to have a deck chair on deck and just watch the other people working and watch the sea, and it was super. We had air-conditioned sports rooms so that even when it was 120 degrees or so outside it was quite cool and I played lots of table tennis and darts.

We had normal, good food – something like salmon as first course, then meat and lovely sweets.

When we were in port in India and Brazil the poverty generally was appalling. In India it was very bad. They used to be starving to death and they'd sit in the gutters by the side of the pavements, whole families, fathers, mothers, tiny children and babies – and do you know, we all ignored them. They'd crouch on the pavements outside the entrance to the luxury hotels we went to and we would step over them and we'd go in and have our elegant food. It was as though they were animals... and yet when I looked at their faces, some of those Indians had more beautiful faces than anyone I've ever seen anywhere in the world. Even though they were probably dying of starvation. Beautifully shaped faces and features, and colouring too. It was shameful, but that was how it was.

For years I was the only woman allowed to go on trips. Then they brought in that the Chief Engineer's wife could go for, say, three months a year and then finally they had to change it ... over the years it was allowed that other wives could go too. I liked being the only woman on the ship because it was a privileged position. It was really nice because when we came into port the crew's first stop would be the first big pub they came to, where they used to get rather sozzled. They would get sentimental and they'd either buy something for me as a present or pinch some odd thing. Once it was embarrassing when the boatswain began to give me money to buy myself a gift. I had to say no, and said the only way I could accept it was to send it to a sea charity such as the Homes for Children of Seafarers.

I was a friend of a lot of them and they used to confide in me and say, 'Now if I tell you something, you won't tell the Master, will you?', and they'd tell me their little moans and groans, especially when they got letters from home with wives very discontented, having to bring up two or three children on their own.

One of the most difficult things about being at sea was missing my son. As he got older he went to a local prep school. I arranged with the headmaster that he could go in as a boarder when I went away and be a day boy when I came home. When I had to say goodbye there would be tears in both our eyes. Later that evening, if it was summer, I'd walk down to his school and peep round sheds and things and see him playing and laughing with his pals. Then I'd know all was well and I could go away.

Well, one of the things that was so marvellous about sailing the sea was it was like a different world. It wasn't like this world that we live in that we are so busy spoiling. There were such beautiful, calm nights out on the Equator and although the ship was so big there wasn't a sound of a ripple. It was total silence. We did have a few hurricanes and I was terrified. I'd go up to the bridge and sit there and not dare say a word to anyone. My husband might give me the odd nod but he was too busy looking after the ship. He had a job to do. One hurricane we were in off the Norwegian coast was very frightening. They tried to batten down everything but of course the noise was incredible. Everything was smashing and people were rolling around and you couldn't do anything. The ship wouldn't only go up and down from midship to aft but it would also roll from side to side and it seemed like it would go flat and fall over.

When we had these tremendous storms I used to huddle somewhere and think to myself wasn't I stupid, why wasn't I at home like other women, shopping, cooking, chatting in peaceful conditions... and then I'd think , oh, I would never have had this life if I'd done that.

I suppose I have had quite a different life from most women. Women have said to me 'You're different from us'. I get on very much better with most men than I do with women because I've learned how to talk to men. Somehow other women's lives, even as a young girl, never appealed to me. I thought first you got married and you have this wonderful hero and after a few months you get stuck and you become a companion and servant and childbearer for your husband... but I suppose that makes a lot of women contented. But never in my life did I feel that way, and nothing would ever part me from my life at sea.

BARBARA LORENTZEN

From the window of her little flat she can just see the Fal estuary and the boats that have played such a great part in her life. Barbara was born in Falmouth, Cornwall, in 1924. From an early age she wanted to go to sea, an ambition which she fulfilled when she joined the WRNS in 1942. After the war Barbara became the skipper of a pleasure boat which took visitors on trips around the Cornish coast, and was one of only a handful of women to do this. Barbara married a merchant seaman in 1948 and had two children. Now divorced, she still loves to spend time on Falmouth quay and is writing a book about her experiences as a wartime Wren. Barbara is also Vice-chairman of the Cornish Coastal Veterans Association.

I was born in the High Street with the beaches and boatyards at the back so I spent most of my childhood playing on the boats and round the beaches and it's just something I've always done. Used to go rowing around, sailing, 'cos we didn't have a sailing boat, but my brother used to rig up an oar and an old sheet and we used to sail around. Well, my childhood revolved around the sea.

As I got older I sort of envied my brother; he joined the merchant navy and I would have loved to have done that and it took the war to give me this opportunity. And so when I was about sixteen and the war had started I decided I would join the WRNS. I'd left school and I had a job – assistant cashier in the grocery stores – and I was taking a walk down on the quayside at Falmouth and I saw this red boat coming in with Wrens as crew. And I thought that's what I wanted to do, so I went down and asked one where do I apply to join.

I had an interview and the officer, she asked me my qualifications and I said I could sail, I could row a boat and I could swim. And then she said 'Have you any relatives in the Navy?' – 'cos this is a point they always ask – so I said 'Well, yes, I've got two uncles attached to the Admiralty'. Which was true because their boats were taken over by the Admiralty, but I didn't say what they were. So she gave me a form to take home and she said 'You're underage, so you've got to get your parents' permission'. And my mother, knowing my ambitions, she agreed right away. Of course Father says 'You make your bed, you lie in it'. So then I had a medical and I just about passed – the doctor said you're too short and you're not big enough... stretch up, you've got to be at least five foot three [1.60 metres], and I was five foot one [1.55 metres]. But within a matter of three of four months I was in the WRNS, as a Boat's Crew Wren, which I was anxious to do.

Barbara Lorentzen (centre) on her pleasure boat off Falmouth in the late 1940s – holidaymakers were surprised to see a woman at the helm.

Then I was sent to Plymouth for what they called 'disciplinary training'. A fortnight of that – we were kitted out with our uniform and we did lots of marching on parade. I was then stationed in Plymouth. I loved it. We were to look after our own boats, clean them, paint them, maintain them, fix anything mechanical that went wrong with them. Our job was to ferry crews backwards and forwards to their boats and lots of other journeys around Plymouth or down to Falmouth. It was special because you were doing an outdoor job, a man's job, and you were at sea. I loved being out there in the fresh sea air. There were different things that happened every day and you had such good companionship.

I remember once I was in the motor launch *Lithia*, we tied alongside a minesweeper waiting to take some maintenance men ashore when I noticed a lot of 'spits' coming up alongside the boat, which I learnt later was machine-gun bullets. And I looked on the minesweeper – they were all there shouting to me. I saw these bombs dropping and then these planes – two of them – made a sweep coming down the river. Then I turned, I dived on board the minesweeper itself on top of a pile of coal. I was smothered in it, and then I heard this terrific bombing. We saw that astern of us was a collier – the bomb had gone right into it and there were men swimming around, shouting, screaming. So we got into *Lithia* and took *Lithia* over to pick them up. A lot of them had broken arms, legs, gashes on their heads... it was all blood, lots of the men were panicking. Whether it was a woman's job or not didn't really matter, we just had to do something, and I can remember pulling this sailor out and I rolled up my jacket and put it under his head. Afterwards there was a luncheon party thrown at the Savoy Hotel in London to present us with a gift to thank us for the rescue. We had to choose whether we wanted a silver compact or a cigarette case. I chose the compact as I didn't smoke. I remember it was my first visit to London and the first time I'd ever been in a hotel.

When the war finished all the married girls were made redundant. Then I saw this advertisement in the local paper of a new firm called 'Seaboat Services' starting up a boat company and they were advertising for a motor mechanic and an ex-sailor or Wren as crew. So I applied and I got a job with them right away, and I had to get a waterman's licence to be a skipper on the pleasure boat. And apparently there was a lot of prejudice there amongst the Water Board, but one local man knew me and lived near the Wrennery where I was. He stuck up for me – he'd seen Wrens handle boats – so I did get my waterman's licence. And I think I was the only woman at that time in the whole of England, I think, that had one, and I was only twenty-one. So I became the skipper of the *Seawave*, with a crew. And there was two boats ... the other one was called *Seahorse*, and that first summer we plied for hour trips around the harbour. We were so busy 'cos a lot of ex-service people were bringing their families down and going for trips around the harbour. Then some days they decided to do day trips to Fowey, Mevagissey, Cadgwith and Looe, Polperro, and I thoroughly enjoyed those long trips out to sea. I was in my element – the rougher the better!

I was really proud to be the only lady skipper on the boats. The passengers were very surprised when they saw me at the wheel, and they were quite delighted. We just had one or two that were a bit dubious and caused a bit of trouble. On one occasion, as soon as I got to the wheel I heard one of the visitors, a man, remark about women being on the wheel, but I ignored it and it was all right. We got down to Helford, and as we were going into the Helford River I was overtaking another motor launch but suddenly this motor launch veered over in front of me for some reason and of course I had to slow down. And I heard this customer start saying 'Oh, she doesn't know the rules of the road, she's doing things wrong' and all that. So we went up the river and things were all right then. But coming back a real wind had got up – it was really blowing a stinker and it was really blowing up the sea. Well, everybody was up forward and the boat, instead of riding over the waves, she was going under 'cos there was too much weight there. So I had to shout for everybody to go back and this man was really shouting his head off – he really was – going on about 'women drivers'. It was the women who went back, they didn't mind. But he wasn't going to move and some of the others weren't going to move and we were really going under the sea. So I decided to turn round and take them back to Port Navis and told them that all who wanted to get off could get off there and catch a bus back to Falmouth. This man got off. So the next morning the company I worked for, they had a meeting and said that I did the right thing.

LIZ DUVILL

She is a quietly spoken, handsome woman who tells her extraordinary story in the sing-song lilt of a true Scottish islander. Liz was born in 1937 and was brought up on Dry Island in the northwest of Scotland, where her father fished for lobster and prawns. When she left school at 17 she begged her father to let her go to sea and she spent the next five years working alongside him on the family boat. She went on to become a nurse and then an art teacher before returning to run the family fishing business when her father died. Liz has been married three times and has seven children and one grandchild. She now lives on the coast overlooking the island where she grew up and, with her son, co-owns several holiday cottages. Her traditional Gobelin highland tapestries, which she creates at home, are sold all over the world.

My family have lived on this island on the northwest of Scotland – tiny little island – since 1884 when my great-grandfather had this vision that it was the place to live. It's a tidal island and you can walk across to it when the tide's out, otherwise it's an island and you have to use boats. Now my mother and father came to live there in 1939 after he left the dray-class yachts and I was two years old, so from the age of two I lived on Dry Island in Gurnock on the northwest of Scotland.

Well, boats were my life. At the age of four and a half I went to school in a boat and dropped my reading book in the sea on day one. Big trouble at school because we had one teacher and she was a very fierce lady! I grew up on the island going to school, the only child, wanting to be a boy, wanting to go to sea, wanting to be a fisherman, *mixing* with the fishermen – much to my father's disgust, I may say, because there were terrific taboos against women which I thought, even at that age, was most unfortunate. I felt that women should be at sea and that women had a place at sea. I just felt a sort of call towards the sea and I felt so aggrieved that I'd been born a girl and not a boy because I felt very strongly that my father would have much more approved of a boy and that he would have taught me about his engines and fishing gear but because I was a girl I was taught nothing. And from a very early age I resented this and I decided to watch and learn on my own, and this I did.

Much later, after I left college, Father had no one to work for him on the fishing because all the young men had gone off to work at the hydro schemes in the 1950s, where they earned lots of money. I said, 'Daddy, can I go to sea with you?'. He said no. So I nagged and I nagged and the fishing was good, it was the summer time, and I said 'Look, we're losing money – why can't I go?'. So we went.

Liz Duvill in the mid-1950s. She was already working full-time with her father in the fishing boat when this picture was taken.

And we were fishing mainly round an island called Longa and out as far as a lighthouse called Ruray Light... very exposed southwesterly aspect. Every day we started off about 6.00 a.m. to set creels, live creels in rotation, bait creels using smelly conger eel cut up with a panga knife, panga-type knife, with two slits in your piece of conger eel to slip into the lobster creel. So we would live-bait, lift – we used a winch, a small winch, and you had to be very careful that you didn't trap your fingers in the winch because that could cause big problems – and we did very well, we were very successful. We would come in and put the lobsters in a big box ready to be shipped off to Billingsgate market.

Now we didn't just fish for lobsters because at that time, in the 1950s, prawns were just coming into fashion. People who went to the Mediterranean ate prawns, they knew about prawns, but really my father before that threw prawns away – they were rubbish, nobody ate prawns. So we started to fish prawns and that was a different system. You were fishing out on mud, not in close to the wild shore where we fished for lobsters, and again the bait was different – we used different, fresher bait for prawns.

Now, when we came in with prawns from the fishing grounds my father would take me back to the island and go on his own to Gurnock pier – where he sold his prawns to a fish salesman – because he didn't want the other fishermen to see that he'd taken, first, his daughter and, second, a woman to sea, so I was left at home. Also it would be very bad for my father to take me over to Gurnock to the pier for then I would be stepping across other people's boats to reach the jetty, because at that time and maybe even still today it is considered very unlucky for a woman even to step across your boat.

But I must tell you now that Father gave me no quarter – that I worked as hard as any young man in dangerous, bad conditions on an exposed shore with a southwesterly aspect. Some of the days we went out it was blowing a full gale because my father had total disregard for the weather. He didn't really wait for calm days and he seemed to think that you got better fishing on bad days anyway, which I believe is true. When the sea is stirred up then fish are more active.

You never feel seasick because you feel afraid. The adrenaline flows and you get this terrific high – you just do not feel seasick, you just feel like working, working, working, getting it over with, getting back home, getting out of here before something happens. Very tiring work. The other aspect was that sometimes bones from the fish would go into your fingers, or if we caught sea urchins – and we don't eat sea urchins in Scotland as the French do – you take the sea urchins out and you get spines from sea urchins in your fingers. Terribly painful. But we didn't wear rubber gloves. I enjoyed it though – I wouldn't have missed it for anything. I think it was one of the experiences in my life whereby I learnt the most. I learnt about the elements, I learnt about the sea, and I loved it.

I was very well aware that I was the only woman going fishing, but in my heart I hoped that being the first locally that this would encourage other young women to go to sea if their husbands or their fathers wanted them to. I wanted to break the taboo because I am not superstitious. I have never been superstitious and I thought it was ridiculous that women – who would probably add to the economy of the place – were driven away or not allowed to work at sea if they wanted to. And I just wanted to change things – and I feel that over the years I have changed things locally a great deal.

After a few years of working with Father I moved away and had children. Well, we were living on a farm on the east coast of Scotland and I used to pray to God that soon we would be able to go and live on the west, beside the sea, where I felt I belonged and where I felt I wanted to bring up my children. And eventually, tragically, we did have that opportunity when one Burns night my father went out for a drink with his friends and then on his return he got into his little boat to row to the island. What happened I don't know because in the morning his body was found six feet under the sea, clutching the seaweed.

We were informed and we came home immediately. And my mother, of course, was in a terrible state... My children were tremendously helpful from the minute they arrived because I had taken the precaution during holidays to teach them how to row and teach them a little bit about boats. And although the eldest was only eleven, he took over; the second boy, who was only eight, seemed to have an instinct to take over the bigger boat. We never sold any of the boats. We went straight to sea and started fishing – that first week after we buried my father we were all at sea. I was ferrying the children to school every day and we were catching lobsters. We carried on the business that my father had started in 1939 with no break and the children just took to the sea as if they had been born there. Oh, it was wonderful to be back, it was wonderful to teach my sons the knowledge I had, albeit limited, about boats, engines, nets, creels... everything I knew I taught them and they were only little. And it is a source of great joy to me that now two of my sons are at sea and one's a very successful fisherman indeed, working out of Lochmaddy in the Outer Hebrides.

6

For Those in Peril

A most powerful and evocative image of shipwreck in the first half of the century is that of the *Titanic*, slowly sinking in the middle of the Atlantic, its lights blazing and its band playing. This most famous of maritime disasters, which occurred back in 1912, still haunts the popular imagination. The horror captures one of our worst fears – to be a passenger on a stricken ship with little hope of rescue. However, the abiding fascination with this and subsequent tragedies involving ocean-going liners has helped to disguise the fact that the great majority of maritime deaths and disasters were of men who worked at sea on fishing and merchant vessels or in the Royal Navy.

In 1914 there were still more than 8000 merchant sailing ships registered in Britain, and those seamen who embarked on voyages in them were taking the greatest risk. The most dangerous trade route was around Cape Horn at the southernmost point of South America, notorious for its storm-force winds and mountainous seas. Many were wrecked on the Horn's inhospitable islands, to die of hunger or cold. Between 1904 and 1908 twenty-six large British sailing ships went missing as they were rounding the Horn, taking with them 59 apprentices and 312 seamen. Steamships and steam trawlers – first introduced in Victorian times – had proved themselves more reliable and safer than sail, and by the 1930s few merchant sailing ships and fishing smacks remained.

A storm at sea. The unpredictable North Sea can produce waves of up to sixty feet high during winter time.

Crews who worked on merchant sailing ships were taking the greatest risk. The most dangerous trade route was around Cape Horn, notorious for its storm force winds and mountainous seas.

Those in distress on the high seas looked to each other for rescue if their ship was going down. Each year the heavy storms in the North Sea produced a new crop of brave deeds and heroes, unseen by the public, as seamen saved the lives of fellow seamen – in a sense they acted as deep-sea lifeboatmen. They were helped by the development of wireless and radio, enabling ships in distress to call for assistance from those nearby. From 1919 all large merchant and passenger ships had, by law, to be fitted with wireless telegraphy. Shipping forecasts also began to be transmitted over the air and were of inestimable value in helping seafarers to avoid the worst storms and conditions.

Some safety measures were initiated to avoid further disasters like the *Titanic*. Shortly after its sinking world shipping lanes were shifted south and ice patrols tracked thousands of icebergs, warning mariners away from dangerous areas. All ships were also required to carry enough lifeboats to hold everyone on board, leading to a boom in the manufacture of ship's lifeboats in the 1910s and

1920s. There were other improvements too – the design of better and safer ships, superior instruction of officers and greater awareness of life-saving methods – all of which helped to reduce the death toll at sea. Peacetime losses of British merchant seamen and fishermen gradually fell from around 1000 each year in the 1900s to around 300 a year by the early 1930s.

It was the coastal waters around the British Isles that formed the main graveyard for ships and men. Britain's rugged west coast lies in the path of some of the worst weather in the world, and to the east the shallow, choppy North Sea can produce waves up to 60 feet high during winter storms. These age-old hazards for the British seafarer provided an important impetus for the formation of

The Margate lifeboat in the 1930s. The Royal National Lifeboat Institution, founded in 1824, was the world's first organized lifeboat service.

the Royal National Lifeboat Institution in 1824, the world's first organized lifeboat service. The aim was to save lives from distressed and wrecked ships. Each lifeboat and lifeboat station was organized locally, paid for by fund-raising and crewed by volunteers, all under the umbrella of the RNLI. By 1900 there were 262 lifeboat stations the length and breadth of the British coastline. The tradition of firing 'maroons', or rockets, to alert the crew and the rush down to the lifeboat station to don yellow oilskins and launch the boat was by then well established.

Most of the lifeboats were based in fishing villages and towns, and most of the crews were fishermen or seamen. Often crews came from generations of the same family, the father handing the helm over to his sons or nephews. The modest heroism of these men who put to sea when other seafarers were running for shelter was responsible for the saving of thousands of lives. In 1933 (a fairly typical year), for example, there were 320 launches to vessels in distress and 406 lives saved. The RNLI rewarded the men who risked their lives with a small fee of a few shillings for a callout, perhaps a pound for a rescue, and the promise of a much-coveted bronze, silver or gold medal for the most courageous deeds. The main reward, though, was the profound camaraderie of those who worked and lived at sea – as is reflected in the stories of one of Britain's most revered lifeboatmen, Dick Evans, who won two gold medals for his daring rescues in the Moelfre lifeboat off the coast of Anglesey.

Before the Second World War most of the work of the RNLI was done in the winter months as fishing vessels and merchant ships were driven aground or on to the rocks by high winds and heavy seas. Sea rescue was very difficult in the early lifeboats. Until the mid-1920s four out of every five RNLI lifeboats were of the pulling or pulling and sailing type – they were driven by oars or oars and sails. This meant they were often slow and difficult to manoeuvre and could only operate fairly close to the coastline. The launching of the lifeboat was also sometimes a difficult and time-consuming business, especially where harbours dried out at low tide or where lifeboat houses were some distance inland. They were often dragged across sand and shingle and propelled into the water by women helpers – sometimes the wives and mothers of the lifeboatmen – or by horses. Arthur Badcock, who began on the Clovelly lifeboat in north Devon in

***Right:* The launching of the Dungeness motor lifeboat in 1933. Motor lifeboats improved the life-saving ability of the RNLI.**

***Overleaf:* The Scilly Isles lifeboat in 1910. At this time all RNLI boats were of the pulling and sailing types.**

R.N.L.B. CHARLES COOPER HENDERSON

1929, remembers how primitive the early rowing and sailing lifeboats were.

'If you were called out in a storm you'd be tossed about like a toy boat... every minute she'd go down flat, her sails would go down in the water, then she'd come up again. And you'd all get submerged – each wave would give you a nasty wallop, water up to your armpits, and it would go up underneath your oilskins and round your waist – you'd be sat in freezing-cold water. Once we were called out to Lundy... we stayed out for 16 hours and I've never been so cold in my life. We were all so wet and so cold we were absolutely numb. When we come in they had to lift us out of the boat, lay us on the beach and stretch our legs and our arms out so we could walk. When I got home Mother made me some hot milk, and I think I spilt most of it I was shaking so badly.'

Motor lifeboats, the first of which began service in 1904, transformed the life-saving capability of the RNLI. They could go faster and farther in worse conditions and save lives that, without them, would have been lost. Before the coming of motor lifeboats no protection was provided for crews, which restricted the time a boat could remain out. Now there were cabins as lifeboats were staying out longer and travelling farther. Fewer crew members were needed as the engines rather than the men provided the power. As the advantages of motor lifeboats came to be appreciated the RNLI fleet was transformed. By the eve of the Second World War it was almost completely motorized. The numbers of pulling and sailing lifeboats declined from 150 in 1925 to 23 in 1938, and the last one – in New Quay in Dyfed – was finally replaced by a motor lifeboat in 1948.

The development of motor lifeboats made the work of the crews safer. There had been periodic disasters with pulling and sailing lifeboats – one of the worst was at Rye, East Sussex, in November 1928, when 17 died – but the loss of lifeboatmen began to decline. Nevertheless there were still major risks. In January 1939 the St Ives lifeboat became the first motor lifeboat of any type to capsize and the lives of seven of the crew were lost – a tragedy that is still vivid in the memories of surviving relatives like Margaret Freeman, who lost her brother.

With the coming of war in 1939 the RNLI was powerless to assist in most sinkings at sea as these tended to occur in mid-ocean – far out of the reach of their lifeboats. One of the main government strategies to reduce the loss of merchant and passenger ships in wartime was the introduction of the convoy system. The theory was that convoys would be protected from the menace of submarine and air attack by an armed escort. In practice, however, especially in the early stages of the war, there were not enough escort ships to do the job properly. Smaller convoys could expect little more than a destroyer and an

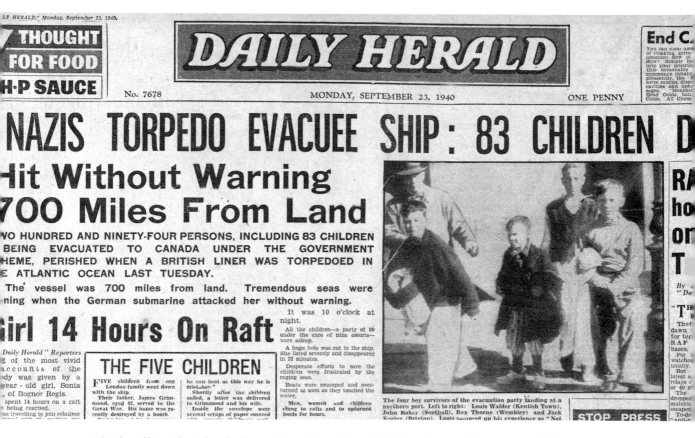

LY HERALD," Monday, September 23, 1940.

No. 7678 MONDAY, SEPTEMBER 23, 1940 ONE PENNY

NAZIS TORPEDO EVACUEE SHIP: 83 CHILDREN D

Hit Without Warning 700 Miles From Land

VO HUNDRED AND NINETY-FOUR PERSONS, INCLUDING 83 CHILDREN BEING EVACUATED TO CANADA UNDER THE GOVERNMENT HEME, PERISHED WHEN A BRITISH LINER WAS TORPEDOED IN E ATLANTIC OCEAN LAST TUESDAY.

The vessel was 700 miles from land. Tremendous seas were ning when the German submarine attacked her without warning.

Girl 14 Hours On Raft

Daily Herald" Reporters

E of the most vivid accounts of the edy was given by a year - old girl, Sonia , of Bognor Regis.

spent 14 hours on a raft being rescued.

as travelling to join relatives

THE FIVE CHILDREN

FIVE children from one London family went down with the ship.

Their father, James Grimmond, aged 42, served in the Great War. His home was recently destroyed by a bomb.

he can beat us this way he is mistaken."

Shortly after the children sailed, a letter was delivered to Grimmond and his wife.

Inside the envelope were several scraps of paper covered

It was 10 o'clock at night.

All the children—a party of 90 under the care of nine escorts—were asleep.

A huge hole was cut in the ship. She listed severely and disappeared in 22 minutes.

Desperate efforts to save the children were frustrated by the raging seas.

Boats were swamped and overturned as soon as they touched the water.

Men, women and children clung to rafts and to upturned boats for hours.

The four boy survivors of the evacuation party landing at a northern port. Left to right: Louis Walder (Kentish Town), John Baker (Southall), Rex Thorne (Wembley) and Jack Keeley (Brixton). Louis summed up his experience as "Not

STOP PRESS

The headline that shocked a nation. A broadcast by King George VI announced that 'The world could have no clearer proof of the wickedness against which we fight than this foul deed.'

armed trawler. And until July 1940 convoys were escorted only to 150 miles west of Ireland – most ships were unescorted for the greater part of the Atlantic crossing. The consequences of this unpreparedness were brought home in September 1940 when the passenger liner *City of Benares*, carrying 83 evacuee children from the bombed cities of Britain to a safe haven in Canada, sank after a submarine attack. Of the 406 people on board 256 were lost, including most of the children. Bess Cummings – then 15 years old – was one of the survivors. She escaped death by clinging to an overturned ship's lifeboat in heavy seas for around 15 hours.

Bess's rescuer was Albert Gorman, an able seaman on the destroyer *Hurricane*, which was in the area at the time and was sent to search for survivors. She was one of several hundred people he rescued from the mid-Atlantic during the

Oil soaked survivors from a torpedoed British ship are rescued after three days in the China Sea in 1944. Four of the sailors died on the voyage home.

war. He would go out on a whaler or motor boat to pick up survivors. It was men from the Royal Navy like George who operated the most effective rescue service on the high seas in the early years of the war – makeshift and ill-equipped though it was.

There was often a long wait for those lucky enough to be rescued at sea, during which time their chances of survival depended on a combination of luck, personal strength and resourcefulness. The merchant seamen and the men of the Royal Navy who found themselves on such missions were generally portrayed as war heroes, their modest stoicism and gritty determination celebrated in countless newspaper reports and newsreels. The popular stereotype was of a long, treacherous journey in a lifeboat, ending in rescue, as in the classic wartime film *Western Approaches*.

The reality of sinking and survival was much more complex, chaotic and brutal – as is revealed in the detailed records of ship and crew casualties kept by the Admiralty and various official bodies during the war. Most ships when hit sank very quickly – the majority within 15 minutes. It was at this time that deaths were most likely to occur, especially if the attack was at night and the evacuation of the ship took place in darkness. The normal experience of abandoning ship was confused and chaotic. Once the crews got away from their ships their chances of surviving were determined largely by the time they had to spend awaiting rescue and the climate. Around a half of those who survived were rescued within two hours and two-thirds within a day. Less than a fifth were in lifeboats or on rafts for more than a week and just three in every hundred were at sea for between three and seven weeks. The death rate among those forced to abandon ship in low temperatures was very high – in the Arctic immersion in the freezing water could lead to death within minutes. It is only through the memories of seamen – like George Field – whose ships were sunk that the true horror and degradation of the battle for survival on the lifeboats and in the sea can be revealed.

The chances of survival of seamen whose ships went down did improve slightly as the war continued. There was increased provision of better, more seaworthy lifeboats on practically all merchant ships and of improved life-saving appliances, such as portable radio transmitters, survival suits and medical kits, for use in lifeboat emergencies. And in 1941 convoy rescue ships were introduced Each was fitted with life-saving equipment and an operating theatre and had a naval medical officer on board. Just 29 rescue ships were provided, however, which meant that they were able to accompany only one in every four convoys.

One of the most important advances made in sea rescue during the last war was that of air–sea rescue. Its development came in response to the huge losses of RAF pilots who bailed out over the English Channel in the first year of the war – over 80 per cent were recorded as missing. More extensive use of inflatable life jackets (known as 'mae wests') and improved dinghies helped, but the key improvement was expanded air search facilities to spot survivors and high-speed motor launches to rescue them. The launches, operated by the Marine Branch of the RAF, improved the ratio of rescues to ditchings to 35 per cent by 1941 and during the course of the war saved more than 14,000 lives. John Huntley worked on RAF sea rescue between 1942 and 1945.

'It got so well organized that we didn't wait to be called out to a plane in trouble. If there was a big raid with a lot of planes going down or coming back over the Channel we were called out in advance and there'd be a line of high-speed launches about a mile [1.6 kilometres] apart, patrolling across the water. We could go quite fast, about 35 knots, and we got so good at it we could reach most planes that ditched within a couple of minutes. You had to because some of the pilots were in a bad state and all they had was a mae west. They wouldn't have lasted long in the cold water. I remember one comic occasion, we tracked a pilot parachuting down and we got to him *before* he landed – he came down on the deck! But he cussed the skipper because he landed awkwardly and broke his ankle.'

The lessons learnt in rapid-response air–sea rescue were applied in the immediate post-war years with the first use of helicopters to save life off the coast of Britain. The RAF and the Royal Navy developed their own helicopter fleets to be used in co-ordination with RNLI lifeboats. Although the early helicopters of the late 1940s could only operate about sixty miles from their base, they had huge advantages over the lifeboat in terms of speed and the ability to search an area. Sometimes they could rescue from vessels that lifeboats could not reach. From the 1950s on helicopters became more sophisticated and played an important role in increasing numbers of emergencies – their use represented the single most significant advance in post-war sea rescue.

The biggest changes in rescue off the British coast since the last war, however, came about as a consequence of the massive increase in the numbers of people who put to sea for pleasure in sailing boats, power boats, canoes and

Abandoning ship in wartime. Life expectancy in the cold waters of the Arctic or North Atlantic was only a few minutes – a place on a raft would improve a seaman's chances of survival.

NORMAN WILKINSON
A FEW
CARELESS WORDS
MAY END IN THIS–
Many lives were lost in the last war through careless talk
Be on your guard! Don't discuss movements of ships or troops

During both world wars there was a massive increase in the loss of life at sea as a result of torpedo attacks from enemy submarines.

dinghies. Many knew little about navigation or tidal movements and, by the 1950s, most of those rescued were pleasure-boaters in distress. The vast majority of callouts now occurred in the summer months, especially during the holiday season. This pattern became even more pronounced as Britain's merchant and fishing fleets went into decline – most of their distress calls had been in the winter storms. The RNLI responded to this new demand by introducing 'inshore rescue boats' in the early 1960s – small, fast, inflatable boats fitted with outboard motors and operated by a crew of just two or three. By 1970 the number of people rescued each year by inshore lifeboats exceeded those rescued by conventional boats, a trend which has continued to the present day. The kind of people that crewed the lifeboats changed too. Once it had been predominantly fishermen and their sons, now it was more mixed with many experienced yachtsmen and pleasure boaters volunteering for duty. It is all a far cry from sea rescue in the makeshift sailing and rowing boats of the first decades of the century, but the principle – the saving of life from shipwreck – remains the same.

DICK EVANS

Dick Evans is the only living lifeboatman to hold two RNLI Gold Medals, the equivalent of a Victoria Cross. Dick was born in Moelfre, on the northeast coast of Anglesey, in 1905. His home is full of reminders of a long career at sea – although all are modestly displayed, as befits this gentle, unassuming man. Dick first went to sea in one of the primitive sailing lifeboats in 1921 when he was only 16. It was the beginning of an association with the RNLI that lasted more half a century and saw him rise to become Coxswain in 1954. A proud Welsh speaker, Dick married Nansi in 1935 and they had three sons, one of whom followed him into the lifeboat service.

It was the ambition of every boy in this village, Moelfre, to be one day made a member of the lifeboat crew. I could row a boat when I was about five. I could swim when I was very, very young. We even played lifeboats with boxes. The old gentleman that kept the post office, he used to have big wooden boxes and he sold them for a shilling [5 pence] – a lot of money then. Well, we put a mast up, made the sail out of sack, put this box sideways to the wind and it would blow over, capsize. Then we'd go out in the 'lifeboat', in another box

Dick Evans pictured when he first went to sea at the age of 16. He went on to become the most highly decorated lifeboatman in the RNLI.

we'd made. So we played lifeboats when we were children.

If the lifeboat was called out we all rushed to the boathouse to see the old lifeboat – pulling and sailing lifeboat. There were fifteen of a crew and we loved watching them going out. They were called out a lot in the old days because we get some terrible seas here with the northerly wind – comes straight between the Isle of Man and Northern Ireland – and very often the sailing ships would get trapped. Quite spectacular to see a ship on her side.

You see, the lifeboat was the centre of all the activities in this little village. And very often the lifeboat would be called out on a Sunday. In those days the chapel would be full and there'd be pandemonium there. Instead of twenty going off to the boathouse to the lifeboat – maybe fifteen crew and five helpers to help get it out – there'd be about 150 going out and the chapel would soon be emptied. There might be a visiting preacher there, you see, didn't know what happened – he thought it was the end of the world!

Well, one day I went out on the lifeboat. I was home on leave from a ship and the maroons went up and I, like the rest of the village boys, rushed to the boathouse. The lifeboat was being launched by the old coxswain, Cox'n Lewis. He said, 'How old are you Richard?'. So I said 'Eighteen'. Well, I was sixteen then, I'd been at sea a while, and he said 'Come aboard'. The proudest moment of my life was walking up the ladder into the lifeboat. And the crew, they all wore beards – that was the fashion in those days. I could hear them saying 'Bloody schoolboy, made a member of the lifeboat crew now'. We had to lower the lifeboat outside the door and get the masts up and there was a hook at the top of the mast that somebody had to climb up to get it down. They had several attempts and failed, then I had a go. It was easy for me and after that I was accepted as a member of the crew. 'Cos every time the lifeboat went out when I was home on leave the old cox'n always called me out.

The old pulling and sailing lifeboat, it wasn't easy by a long way. There were six oars each side of the lifeboat, six blue and six white. Well, there were so many in the crew didn't understand English – they could only speak Welsh – the coxswain would say 'Back blue, forward white'... they understood that. But it was very hard work because the oars were very, very big and heavy, your hands would be bleeding holding on to them. We used the oars to get as near the casualty as possible, get a rope aboard and then pull the lifeboat closer and the casualties jumped aboard.

And it got terribly cold in the old lifeboat, you know, because there was no shelter. You're in the open and the sea lashed right over you. You were drenched from the moment you went down the slipway, which was greased to gather speed, and when it hits the water the sea comes right over you. And out at sea the water came over you... a big sea could come and wash you overboard. Course, it's always bad weather when the lifeboat goes out – you go out to sea when it isn't fit for a ship to be out. So you had a rope to hold on to and you were gripping it so tight it damaged your hands. You were so cold and wet all the time we took a bottle of rum in the lifeboat with us that was a hundred per cent proof. It was only for when you were near dead it was so strong!

The first motor boat we had, just before the war, it was a bit easier. You had more shelter from the sea, you could go faster and it was very much easier to get alongside a ship. Then the war came. That made it difficult again because there were no lights on any ships, they daren't put a light on. You had to be careful you didn't have a collision. The lighthouses only flashed now and again and there were no lights on at shore so very often you weren't sure where you were going. And 'twas very difficult to get a crew here then because they were all at sea in the merchant navy, so 'twas a very old crew. Today you have to finish at 55, but goodness me, there were some over 80 on the boat then!

I became a coxswain in 1953. I was very proud of being coxswain of the Moelfre lifeboat, very proud, and I am proud today of every life I've helped to save. After I became coxswain I fully realized the responsibility that was on me. Because it was not only your own life you risked, it was the life of the crew as well, you see. The honorary secretary of the local lifeboat always used to leave it to me to make the decision whether to take the lifeboat out, and generally it would be in a bad sea. Many a coxswain has lost lives. And if I'd made a mistake and lost my own life as well as the crew's lives everybody would be up in arms. 'The fool, he should never have attempted it.' I knew very well at times I was attempting the impossible, but you see I've always prayed in the lifeboat. I believe in prayer; I asked God to help me. My prayer only consisted of three sentences: 'Please God guide me'; things becoming worse – 'Please God help me'; things becoming impossible – 'Please God save us'. And I believe that some power not understood by the biggest scholar in the world has helped me during my time in the lifeboats. I shall always believe that.

I was in the house here with my wife helping her to make lunch as usual and the wind 'twas blowing very hard. I knew there was some ships in the bay so I decided to go down to the boathouse. I could hardly stand on my feet, and it was blowing so hard I had to hold on to the rails on the side of the road leading to the lifeboat station. I was horizontal the wind was blowing me so much, and when I got to the boathouse there was only three of my crew there. I couldn't get in touch 'cos all the telephone wires were down – covered with hay and straw from the farms around here. There was slates off houses went flying like snowflakes. I had four crew instead of seven. You're not supposed to go out unless you've got a full complement of crew, but I decided to launch with four men against the rules. I'd broken every rule in the book, anyway – several times. It was terrible. My grandfather taught me all the seamanship I knew but he never told me how to cope with this kind of sea. It was a boiling mass of fury. I tied myself down to the wheel – I had to or I'd have been washed overboard – packed my gallant crew into the little shelter on the boat and proceeded round the island to the ship.

The ship, the *Hindley*, wasn't far from the boathouse. But she had no cargo aboard and she was like a balloon on the water. It took a long time for me to get anywhere near her. Then I heard a faint cry on the wireless: 'Can you save us, lifeboat.' And that gave us something… a tremendous thrill went through my body. And then I asked God to help me and I felt a renewed strength when I had the wheel in my arms. I realized that the only way to rescue those men was to drive the lifeboat on to her and hope for the best and that's what I did. But the wind velocity was one hundred and four mile an hour [167 kilometres per hour] – nobody alive had known a wind of that velocity – and to anyone who knows the sea what I was doing was suicidal. The first time I took the lifeboat up to the side of the *Hindley* two men jumped aboard. Then I took another chance and drove the lifeboat on again… and the coastguard said I did this twelve times. I wouldn't know.

But eventually there was one man left – he was hanging on to a rope on the side of his ship. Now a coxswain of a lifeboat has got some very cruel decisions to make. Would it not be wiser for me to save the lives of the seven men I already had on board and the crew, and my own life, rather than risk losing them all to save that one man? But somehow I could not leave him. He could be a father like us, he could love his family the same as I loved mine and I certainly didn't want him to die. I took another desperate gamble this time because she was very close to the rocks – and this time the lifeboat was lifted right up to the rail of the ship. If it had touched the rail I wouldn't be here today, but miraculously another wave washed it off and to my amazement this man was thrown on to the deck of the lifeboat.

The journey from the *Hindley* to the lifeboat house was hell itself for me. The sea was worse than a lion roaring. It was one big, huge wave, snarling along. And when we came by the slipway there was hundreds of people now down and they were shouting 'She's on the rocks', and in no time the *Hindley* was broken in two, so you have an idea how lucky I was. And I sat on the slipway and I realized my eyes were bleeding where I'd been rubbing the salt off, where the sea had been lashing into my eyes. And I felt myself... 'Yes, I'm alive'. I thought it was impossible. If I hadn't rescued those eight men they would be drowned. Now, should that have happened I wouldn't be the hero they made me – I would be looked down on, my life wouldn't be worth living. That's what a lifeboat is about, you've just got to do your best. But I'll always maintain that I'm a very lucky man.

MARGARET FREEMAN

Margaret was born in 1905 a few doors away from the fishing cottage in St Ives, Cornwall, where she now lives. The daughter of a fisherman, as a child she would help mend nets with her three brothers and two sisters. She married William Freeman, also a fisherman, in 1926 and they had two children. Margaret almost became a widow in 1939 when the St Ives lifeboat capsized with the loss of seven men, one of whom was her brother John. Margaret's husband was the only survivor and he was awarded the RNLI Bronze Medal. Frail and softly spoken, Margaret is still haunted by the events of that night nearly 60 years ago.

I grew up in St Ives and I remember when the rockets went off and everybody just ran – women as well as men would drop what they were doing and go down to the front. In those days the lifeboat had to be pulled out by hand and Mr Phillips and his son, they were in the shafts, just like horses. They were very strong men. There was a rope each side of the lifeboat and that would be hauled along by crowds of youngsters. Anybody would help, and even if the men had their suits on they'd go up to their necks to pull her out.

Margaret Freeman and her husband William on their wedding day in 1926.

Sometimes it was perhaps crabbers in the bay needed help or a steamer would come in with someone sick and the lifeboat would take a doctor out... and there were always crowds watching. Ycs, the lifeboat was part of St Ives, wasn't it.

My brother John lived with my grandparents in the big house and they reared John and sent him to the grammar school and when he got a bit older he went to sea with the Haines Steamship Company. He was a single man and he was great fun, laughing and joking all the time. That's how I remember him.

Well... the night of the great disaster the weather was horrific. The sea was touching the sky. It was really terrible and the wind was so bad that it was ripping off all the slates, the wind was so strong that you couldn't stand up in the street and the sea was roaring.

My eldest little girl was about nine then and was very seriously ill and my father and brother John had just left our house. As they went down the steps John looked back at me and it seemed as if he was going to cry – and I never saw him again. I went back to bed with my little girl, and I presume John and my father went down to check the boat. They knew that something was going to happen. Now William, my husband, went to look out over the bay from the bedroom window and he said it was terrible conditions. I told him, 'If the lifeboat do go off you aren't going nowhere – look what you got here ill in bed'. He wasn't a member of the crew, but of course most of them were volunteers. I remember him taking his legs out of his trousers and the maroons went off and he put them straight back on again. So I said to William, 'Go on down to help with the lifeboat but don't go out on it', and he went.

Later on that evening I went down to the lifeboat and a cousin of mine came along with a life jacket, but he changed his mind so William put his hand out and took the life jacket. Course I was very upset then. And I hadn't realized what the sea was like 'cos it was so terrible – there was crowds of people all round 'cos all the women came out the same as the men when anything like that happened. I gave him my hat and I took his cap and Matthew said, 'Oh, she's all right, the boat, she's safe as houses' – but I never saw Matthew or Edgar ever again. And I turned round and went home, 'cos of my children. I went back to wait, putting his clothes on air – 'cos you did that when yer men went out, all dry clothes waiting for them 'cos you knew they were going to be wet up to their necks and I remember kneeling down to ask the Lord to bring him in safe and sound.

At about seven o'clock Sunday morning my father came round and I slipped down to the wharf. On the way a woman said 'Oh Margaret, isn't it awful'. I said, 'Don't tell me anything about the lifeboat, my man's in her'. I ran down to the wharf crying and someone else told me the lifeboat was gone – my husband was all right. I ran home to Mother and told her and she went 'cos she knew John, my brother, was in her. So many people lost brothers or sons. That time was absolutely dreadful. William was in the farmhouse over Gwithian and came back all bruised and bleeding and battered, hardly able to walk and supported by men. We put our arms round each other and cried.

It was a long time really before William could tell me what happened on board but I know he couldn't have the light out when we went to bed. He couldn't bear to be in the dark. He said he wished with all his heart that when the boat got outside the harbour she'd turned over then because everybody would have had a chance to get ashore. They got out round the Head and she met in with a big sea and turned her over. Now she was a self-righter, so in a minute she come up again, but skipper was gone and John was gone and Edgar. She was at the mercy of the sea... and Dick tried to go forward but she turned over again, losing Dick. It was William and Jack and Matthew left. Matthew wedged his hand down in the canopy so if she turned over again he would still be there, and she did. William said he got up on a flat rock, but he said Matthew and Jack flew over his head and they was gone and so he started to scramble ashore. Poor William, he suffered terribly for months and he wasn't able to go out. He was disfigured, you know.

John, my brother, was picked up Friday, which was nearly a week after, and he was taken home to my mother's... but he didn't look a bit like John, never had any hair, all washed off. But I tell 'ee this, I don't think there was an able man in the town who didn't go looking for their bodies and they knew whereabouts they would be because the tide was right in to Gwithian, see, and they would be carried there. The coxswain and William Barber was picked up the next day. But they went over the sand, d'you see, and they'd see a mound and they'd scrape away and there would be one of them. Edgar was picked up three weeks after and his body was carried up the coast a bit. He was picked up and he still had his jersey on, they said.

Well, of course the town was out for the funerals but my mother was unable to go. It was a terrible thing, the fishing community was devastated. We were all interlocked, you see. You felt for each other – it affected us all.

BESS CUMMINGS

Bess was only 15 when she boarded the *City of Benares* at Liverpool with her younger brother Louis in 1940. The ship was to take them to Canada, away from the bombs that were falling on British cities and towns. It was a voyage that was to change her life forever. After the war Bess trained to become a teacher, eventually retiring as headmistress of a large primary school. She married Jeff in 1947. Bess now leads a very happy, busy life at her home in Gloucestershire. She is a member of The Children of Benares, the association that keeps survivors of the disaster in touch.

In 1940 things were getting quite dangerous in large cities, particularly in London and Liverpool. During the war people were getting very concerned about the fate of their children, and when the government first announced the scheme to evacuate all the young children from major cites to friendly countries like Canada, Australia and New Zealand the scheme was instantly popular.

My parents heard of this scheme – they too, like many others, were very concerned because my brother and I had missed so much in the way of education. We were also subjected to nightly bombings, and so when the scheme was announced they asked us if we would like to go to Canada. We were absolutely thrilled – so thrilled I think perhaps my mother felt quite put out that we were so willing to leave her. The process started to get us on this scheme and it took a long time, but by September we had letters to say we were accepted and we should be ready to embark at very short notice.

We'd imagined we'd be able to take almost anything, but a letter came which said we must only have attaché cases. My brother wanted to take his entire train set, but that was a non-starter, so my father let him take the engine

Bess Cummings, as she was seen in a national newspaper, recovering from her ordeal after the sinking of the *City of Benares*.

and wrapped it up in a pair of socks and put it inside the case. And then the letter came and it said to be ready to take the children to Euston station and from there they would be going to an unknown port. Well, when we got there it was Liverpool, and we were housed overnight in a Liverpool orphanage. We were all war children and we were used to all kinds of things happening to us. People forget how children react and it was not dangerous to us, it was all great fun – an adventure. Then we went off in the morning to see the ship and there it was, the most beautiful thing I'd ever seen – inland children hardly ever got a chance to see a liner, and this one just glowed with beautiful things. The ship was called the *City of Benares* and she was only four years old. As we approached the gangway our stewards were waiting for us and they all bowed to us and called us 'little sirs' or 'madams'. You can imagine the exhilaration!

We soon settled down into the shipboard routine. We had, of course, our fire drill and our lifeboat drill. These two things went on daily. In fact, we knew that we could find our lifeboat even in the dark. We had to wear life jackets, even in the cabins, because of course anything might happen at any time. They were uncomfortable – they were great cork things that sat on your chest. The days went by in a haze of wonderful excitement. We had a playroom, a school room and games on the deck. And all the children became very friendly with each other.

The weather had been extremely good and the sea was calm, but around the 17th of September the weather seemed to change and also a change in the way the ship was moving. Now instead of sailing along calmly as it had been, it started to roll. Well, all that food suddenly became much less interesting! That night the captain sent down orders that no one must be on deck, that the weather was in fact going to be much worse and all children must be in their cabins.

The storm raged and the waves became mountainous. The ship rolled tremendously from one side to another and then there was the most tremendous explosion. It was actually two torpedoes. One had missed its target and had landed elsewhere and the other had gone into the ship. It hit just below deck where the children were sleeping and that meant the children were shot out of their beds by the force. Of course the furniture fell about and the bunks went upside down. The ship was sinking fast and it was impossible to get up to our lifeboat deck. I started off going down a corridor with my big life jacket on and as I walked down the passageway, so the chasm opened up in front of me. The entire deck disappeared and all I could see looking down was a great deal of machinery being covered with water. I was dragged away and led around a different way.

The entire ship was at an angle so all the boats that were supposed to take us away to safety were dangling at the same angle. As we were pushed into the boats they were becoming top-heavy, and as the lifeboats touched the ocean, so the water came over and filled them. You see, the boats were so top-heavy they rolled over and everybody inside was thrown out. Some children hardly managed to get to boats at all. There wasn't absolute panic on deck. Nobody screamed, nobody made a lot of fuss.

Everybody was so very busy and, you see, they had to concentrate. There was very little time because the boat was sinking so fast. The weather was horrendous – dreadful rainstorms and the darkness of the night. It all came together in a dreadful fantasy.

I was really worried about my brother as I didn't know where he was and I thought about what my father had said, about looking after him, but that was really difficult as he was on the other side of the ship.

Then, as the lifeboat was launched sideways, many people drowned. The water came over the top and drenched everybody – children, adults – you see, the little children had no chance because they actually drowned in the water in the lifeboat. Older children had water up to their chests. Adults had water up to their middles and everybody sat in this waterlogged state. As the lifeboat tried to right itself people tried desperately to help by moving the gear in the lifeboat, but they could not shift it.

Meantime that enormous, beautiful ship was sinking fast and we began to feel the undertow and we knew our time was very short to get away. The undertow fortunately didn't affect our boat, but we watched many others that just disappeared. People were jumping then from the ship down into the water hoping to find a raft. It was a terrible sight to see people that we knew jumping from the decks into the ocean with nothing to save them. Our lifeboat got away from the ship and went upside down and everyone was flung out into the water.

The waves were mountainous – it was terrifying.

My father had always taught me to swim in the sea and one day he said to me, 'If you get into trouble in the water you will go down, down and down, and then you'll start to come up and that's when you start your strokes'. As I went down I could hear my father's words. It was like going down into an Alice-in-Wonderland tunnel, green, grey and then black, and then coming up into the dark, into complete blackness – by now the ship had gone down. As I came up my hands touched the sides of the lifeboat – which was now upside down, so I caught the keel and I clambered my way up on to it. I hung on to the keel, which was see-sawing about of course. Originally there had been about fifty of us; now there were about twenty and they'd all done the same as me.

There was a full-scale force-nine gale blowing but we hung on – but gradually I saw people just slipping away, they just gave up hope. Now, I was fifteen, and opposite to me, hanging on too, was another young girl called Beth, and hanging on to the stern an Indian seaman who had tied himself to the gear. And as the night progressed we were the only three left.

Beth and I had absolute faith in the Royal Navy and that they would look after us. We also had strong motivation – you see Beth wanted to get back to her mother who was a widow and alone and I had to get back to prove to my mother and father that I had tried to look after my brother. We had a bond, and in spite of everything happening around us we were determined to hang on.

We had drifted away from the scene of the disaster, but it was still like a scene from a nightmare. Odd pieces of furniture floated by – you could see the rocking horse from the nursery that the little ones were playing on. It was a very difficult experience. The only way we could be saved was to hold on tight. Our hands locked on to that lifeboat, and as the waves came and tipped up and down our bodies were lifted and flung down on to the side of the lifeboat. Eventually we felt no pain because we were so battered and our fronts were just like jelly. Sometimes I think about it and wonder, how did we manage, how did two young girls survive under those dreadful conditions? It just shows how strong the survival instinct is. We were young and optimistic and strong. We were actually rather plump, and this helped to insulate us against the cold.

As the night wore on we consoled ourselves with one thought: when the dawn comes we shall be able to see where we are and there will be other people in boats and rafts and maybe even a plane in the sky to rescue us. Meanwhile the Indian seaman had become quite delirious. He was crazy with fear and was calling Allah to help him. Of course, we couldn't help because we needed our hands to hold on to the boat.

When the dawn came we were tremendously disappointed. It came in streaks of yellow and green across the sky… the clouds were still scudding past but there was this unearthly yellow light, and in the light of this we looked around to see nothing. There we were, two girls, mid-Atlantic, on the top of a very dangerous-looking lifeboat, upside down, with one delirious Indian for company. We were holding on tight but it was remorseless. The waves continued to batter us and by this time our tongues, mouths and gums were swollen and our eyes began to close. We started to hallucinate. I saw strange things like a tray of food descending from the sky and Beth said she saw huge fish.

As the sky darkened we realized we were into evening again and I knew this was make or break time and that we were close to death. And as I looked across the horizon I saw a very, very small dot. It was moving fast – it was a Royal Navy destroyer. As it came nearer and nearer the most tremendous noise was coming from it. It turned out to be the entire crew of the *Hurricane* yelling and shouting at us to stay there and hang on. The men on board that ship had been picking up dead children all day. To see two girls still alive and hanging on to an upturned boat seemed to them to be a total miracle. The captain had been absolutely wonderful because he had been told by one of his men that some small object was on the horizon and instead of turning back – as they ought to have been doing because they were running out of both fuel and time – he ordered more time to search. And so he sent down an order for a long boat, a whaler, to be put out with some strong men and a very experienced coxswain who would lead them to us. They couldn't come close themselves – you see, if the destroyer had come alongside us he would have upset the boat and they couldn't risk that. But sending down a rowboat in that horrendous weather was no mean feat.

As the men rowed closer we were constantly exhorted to hold on, which was ironic really as we'd been hanging on for so long! When they tried to get us off our hands were stuck, were locked into position, and even now I can remember being forced to let go and the huge sense of relief – because we were very near collapse. We were wrapped in rugs and placed like precious cargo into this little boat. We were given rum, and as we approached the destroyer the entire crew shouted and cheered. We were cared for like precious jewels by the young surgeon, who had previously picked up three young children – all of whom died, so I guess we were his reward.

I didn't recover as quickly as Beth because I was so worried about my brother and how I would tell my parents. Kindly sailors tried to reassure me, but I was really worried. One day, sailing back to Scotland, the captain came to my cabin and said, 'Sit up Miss, I've brought you a present', and he revealed my brother. So we were reunited after our terrible ordeal and I began to get better very quickly.

ALBERT GORMAN

Born in Clerkenwell, London, in 1912, Albert Gorman joined the Royal Navy at the age of 17 and served throughout the British Empire. He is a powerful-looking man with huge hands and a variety of tattoos acquired in distant ports during his years at sea. Albert was invalided out of the Navy in 1946 and became a builder before working as Security Supervisor at Shell UK's London office. He lives in Hampshire with his wife, Vera, whom he married in 1939. They have three children. Albert was a 28-year-old seaman on board HMS *Hurricane* when he played a key role in the rescue of survivors – including Bess Cummings – from the *City of Benares* in 1940.

I got detailed to a destroyer called the *Hurricane* and our main job was to go and hunt U-boats in the Atlantic. So out we went, but in the first four or five months we didn't sink any U-boats – we didn't even see a U-boat – and we certainly never took any prisoners. But what we did do was pick up about 900 people from the sea whose ships had been torpedoed by U-boats.

Our most traumatic rescue, in my opinion, was the *City of Benares*. We got a signal – it must have been early in the morning on the 18th of September 1940 – saying that this ship had been torpedoed and we were to go and render any assistance. We were then some 400 to 500 miles [650–800 kilometres] west of Ireland and she was 200 miles away so we started to go towards her. And the sea started to get up and we had to slow down a bit because we would smash the ship up. Eventually I suppose about four o'clock in the afternoon we came to the allocated spot where she

Albert Gorman as a young Petty Officer in 1942. In September 1940, Albert played a key role in the rescue of survivors from the *City of Benares*, one of whom was Bess Cummings.

was sunk. And there was nothing. Not a single thing. No rubbish, no boats, no nothing, and of course we all looked and we were a bit devastated. Then the skipper said 'I'm going to do a box search twenty miles up, twenty miles down, twenty miles across,' he said, 'and go until we find it'.

And we were on the last leg of this search when we saw a lifeboat. Sitting on this upturned lifeboat was a sailor. He had his uniform on, his hat on, and we called to him and asked him where was the people, where was the survivors? And he pointed and we left him – and his face, complete devastation! I spoke to him afterwards and he said 'When you turned away and left me', he said, 'I thought, "Oh my God, no!"'. He had at one time twelve women in that boat, all in their nightclothes, and they were so terrified, he said, they wouldn't get the oars out, and eventually the rough seas knocked 'em off and he ended up on his own. We picked him up right at the very end. So we went off in the direction in which he pointed.

And there was the boats. I think there must have been eleven boats. Anyway, we lowered our rescue boats. There was a motor boat and I was in the whaler – I was coxswain and I had four good oarsmen. And the first one I saw was an upturned boat. These lifeboats looked very small in the sea but they're very large vessels really – they can hold up to 40 people. Any rate, on this upturned keel was this lascar seaman, and then I saw two heads and I went and pulled over to them and I realized they were two females, two young girls, and I saw these two pathetic figures hanging on to the lifelines of the upturned boat. I didn't think it possible that two girls could survive after all those hours in the cold Atlantic, and they were still alive. It was unbelievable. My first thoughts was get 'em out of that water fast as we could. So taking much, much care I got the whaler alongside the upturned lifeboat. The sea was getting up and we had to be careful not to hit the lifeboat in case it collapsed and sunk and they would have been killed. We did this and I jumped on to the lifeboat, picked up first one girl, took her back to the whaler, then the second girl. And the look on their little faces! How they survived I will never know.

Well, then we went to another boat. It was upright but it was full of water, and the thing about this boat – I shall never forget it – there must have been 24 people in this boat and they were all dead. I had a young seaman with me, and when we jumped out the whaler into this boat he picked up a small child in a blue siren suit and obviously the child was dead and I said to him, put it down, I said, we're only looking for live ones, and he swore at me and he put the child back. And we went and had a look in the stern sheets and sitting on the port side facing inboard was a young woman, very attractive girl, and as the boat rolled with the water that was almost up to the gunwales her head was moving. And as the water rolled it lifted her skirts up and I could see her knees, and on both her knees was two big holes in her stockings, and I don't know why but I thought to myself, 'Oh, she won't like that'. And then I expected her to speak to me but she didn't, so I picked up her right hand – I was trying to find a pulse – and as I did I saw her left hand and on her left hand was a huge diamond ring, an engagement ring, and a brand new wedding ring. And I tried to find a pulse, but no, she was dead. We then got called by the ship: 'Any survivors?', and I yelled back, 'They're all dead, sir'. 'Leave 'em', he said, so we pulled away from this boat and as I turned round and looked at this girl her eyes were still open and it seemed that she was still looking at me and I never forgot that. It was most traumatic.

We went round and we picked up many others. And the mood seemed to brighten up – all the crew got a bit more cheerful when we'd established the fact that there was no more out there in the boats dead and we'd got all the live ones. The idea was that when you got them all aboard give them a tot of rum, sip the rum, warm them up. This they did. And then another chap and myself had the job of bathing all these females aft. There was only one bathroom aft and the men and boys were taken for'ard and they had the usual bucket to wash down. And some of these we washed were young girls and married women...

All the ship's company mixed in to help the survivors; there was nothing provided, only from us. Everybody – stokers, signalmen, petty officers, seamen – they all gave underclothes, clothing, anything for them to put on after they'd been bathed. Now I think I can honestly say that in the ten months that we picked up most of these survivors we must have given our underclothes four or five times. We never got 'em back. We were never compensated by the Admiralty for these, never. But we put these girls and these boys in all sorts of funny rigs, which was good because some of the boys were dressed as sailors in suits that didn't fit them and it made them laugh. It cheered them up, and this is always a good thing when you've lost your ship – you want cheering up and you want something to make you laugh, which they did. The food, we had to give 'em our food because you don't carry any extra food for survivors and nobody queried it. You simply made them tea and coffee and cocoa and corned-beef sandwiches – destroyers live on corned beef and biscuits. They put the youngest survivors in cabins, two or three to a bunk, and the rest of them were put down into the wardroom and laid on the carpet. At that time we weren't hunter–killers, we were the lifeboatmen of the high seas.

GEORGE FIELD

Rarely a day goes by when George doesn't think of his wartime experiences. After a brief spell in the merchant navy he joined the Royal Navy as a Sub-Lieutenant in early 1941, when he was 27. As he tells his dramatic story he becomes highly animated and emotional. George says he still dreams about those who died when his ship, HMS *Audacity*, was torpedoed while returning in convoy from Gibraltar in December 1941.

I was sat in a chair reading a book and about a quarter to nine at night there was this fantastic explosion. I knew immediately it was a torpedo. My chair was flung across the room and hit the bulkhead just like a dodgem car. Everybody was fighting to get to their life jackets. But I couldn't see the point of rushing. I knew that this one torpedo wasn't going to put her down in seconds so I just sat there in this chair. I undid my reefer jacket and underneath I had my life jacket already on. And I blew up my life jacket.

What had happened, the first torpedo had hit the rudder and so the rudder went over to starboard slightly and the ship, we went round in a great big circle. It took about three-quarters of an hour, and we gradually came back to where the sub was on the surface. And he couldn't believe his luck! He just sat on the surface and put two more torpedoes into the bow, then two more to follow. I was underneath the flight deck, on the deck below, and I watched these torpedoes coming – and you're hypnotized by the wake of the torpedoes in the sea... it's pitch black and all you can see is the phosphorous wake of these torpedoes. And when they hit I just held on to the stanchion and went over with the ship. She went right over to the starboard side, then the other two hit and it blew a quarter of the ship off for'ard. And then thousands of tons started coming for'ard.

Me having been in the merchant navy I knew what a ship will put up with and do, which was more than an awful lot of the young fellows on the ship. They were young lads from farms – never been on a ship before – and not knowing that the ship would go over on the starboard a lot of them drowned then by the ship leaning over. I waited for her to come back and I realized it was time to get over the side. I put my hand on a locker and there was a watchman's oilskin and I put it on.

The big problem when I went over the starboard side, there was hundreds of bodies in the sea and you can lose your life landing on those bodies and so you prayed that you would hit a piece of the sea where there were no bodies. And then as the ship laid over the fighters broke their moorings and they rolled down the ship's side on to the carley floats. And the screams from those people and the shouting, 'Save me', and kids, young lads, crying for their mothers.

You couldn't really swim, but I had to get as far away from the ship before she actually went under because if you're sucked down you're sucked so far your lungs burst and you come to the surface and that's it. So I got as far as I could away from her. The oilskin I'd put on definitely saved my life. I'd buttoned it, it had storm-proof cuffs and came right down to my feet so that when I went into the water the water went up inside it and my body heated it to a certain extent. Well, the weather was ten below at that time and that's what killed most of them.

I began to think there was something in religion after all and I prayed to God, not verbally, but in my mind, to save my life. And I had all sorts of strange thoughts... why should God save the life of a nobody like me? Then after about three hours the weather started getting up and you're drawn up by the waves and when the top of the wave breaks it hits you and it pushes all the breath out of your body, then you slide back down the back of the wave again and you're picked up again.

Then all of a sudden this fellow got hold of me and got my neck in the crook of his arm. And through sheer panic a fellow in the water would hang on to anything, and the power that they can find by panic in their muscles can literally choke you to death. And I couldn't get at him to push him off and I realized that unless he would let go I was doomed, I was going to die with him. So I pulled myself under the water as best I could and he'd let go to get to the surface and when he came to and he's in front of me I punched him and kicked him off. I'm not proud of the fact, but I had to fight for my life... and he just floated away. Then I was washed against this other fellow and he tried to hold on to my shoulder, and I'm trying to punch and fight him off, and he gradually worked down the oilskin coat I had on and he pulled one shoe off, but I punched him off.

By this time I'd really had it – my eyes were almost closing with the burning of the fuel oil that was in the water and I'd taken fuel oil down my lungs. And I dropped off, believe it or not, and when I came to I was vomiting because of the fuel oil I'd taken down. I really thought I was finished.

But I saw this light – only a tiny little pinprick – and as I was washed further and further towards it I realized it was a corvette. And she was in the troughs of these big waves. And I realized I had a chance of being saved and I shouted out, 'Don't leave me, don't leave me'. Anyway, as I got nearer she was lifted by the waves – and I'm down in a trough and I could see all the underneath side of her, then she'd drop down in a trough and I'm lifted up by a wave and I could look right down on top of her deck. Then I realized as I was washed nearer unless I got to her when she was level with me, if I went underneath she'd come down on top of me, and I really panicked then. But fortunately the wave pushed me against her side and she had a scrambling net and I dug my arm into it and I just hung there. I was just finished. And the chief officer pulled me on deck and I laid on the deck. And I heard the steward saying 'He must be the last one sir'. Then when I came to they put rum in my mouth and it made me vomit immediately. And it took me twelve hours to thaw out.

Further Reading

Adams, Caroline *Across Seven Seas and Thirteen Rivers*. London: Centerprise, 1987.

Bailey, Chris Howard *The Battle of the Atlantic: The Corvettes and their Crews, an Oral History*. Stroud, Glocs: Alan Sutton, 1994.

Bailey, Chris Howard *Down the Burma Road: Work and Leisure for the Below Deck Crew of the Queen Mary*. Southampton: Southampton City Council, 1990.

Barnett, Corelli *Engage the Enemy More Closely: The Royal Navy in the Second World War*. London: Hodder & Stoughton, 1991.

Beardow, Keith *Sailors in the RAF: The Story of the Marine Branch of the Royal Air Force*. Yeovil, Somerset: Patrick Stephens, 1993.

Butcher, David *Living from the Sea*. Reading: Tops'l Books, 1982.

Carew, Anthony *The Lower Deck of the Royal Navy 1900–1939*. Manchester: Manchester University Press, 1981.

Cockcroft, Barry *The Fatal Call of the Running Tide*. London: Hodder & Stoughton, 1995

Dyson, John *Business in Great Waters*. Edinburgh: Angus and Robertson, 1977.

Ekberg, Charles *Grimsby Fish*. Buckingham: Barracuda, 1984.

Ereira, Alan *The Invergordon Mutiny*. London: Routledge, 1981.

Faith, Nicholas *Classic Ships, Romance and Reality*. London: Boxtree, 1995.

Festing, Sally *Fishermen: A Community Living from the Sea*. Newton Abbot: David and Charles, 1977.

Frost, Diane *Ethnic Labour and British Imperial Trade*. London: Frank Cass, 1995.

Gill, Alec *Village within a City: The Hessle Road Fishing Community of Hull*. Hull: Hull University Press, 1986.

Glenton, Bill *Mutiny in Force X*. London: Hodder & Stoughton, 1986.

Gregson, Paddy *Ten Degrees below Seaweed: A True Story of World War 2 Boats' Crew Wrens*. Braunton, Devon: Merlin Books, 1993.

Howell, Colin, and Twomey, Richard (eds) *Jack Tar in History, Essays in the History of Maritime Life and Labour*. New Brunswick: Aedensis Press, 1991.

Hugill, Stan *Sailortown*. London: Routledge, 1967.

Keegan, John *The Price of Admiralty*. London: Hutchinson, 1988.

Kennedy, Paul *The Rise and Fall of British Naval Mastery*. London: Allen Lane, 1976.

Knox-Johnston, Robin *Cape Horn*. London: Hodder & Stoughton, 1994.

Lane, Tony *Grey Dawn Breaking*. Manchester: Manchester University Press, 1986.

Lane, Tony *The Merchant Seaman's War*. Manchester: Manchester University Press, 1990.

Lynch, Don *Titanic: An Illustrated History*. London: Hodder & Stoughton, 1995.

Madge, Tim *Long Voyage Home: True Stories from Britain's Twilight Maritime Years*.

London: Simon and Schuster, 1993.

The Sea. *Oral History Journal*, vol. 19, no. 1, Spring 1991. (Department of Sociology, University of Essex)

Seligman, Adrian *The Voyage of the* Cap Pilar. London: Seafarer, 1993.

Sherwood, Marika Race, nationality and employment amongst Lascar seamen 1600–1945. *New Community*, vol. 17, no. 2, January 1991.

Smithies, Edward, and Bruce, Colin *War at Sea*. London: Constable, 1992.

Stewart, Jean Cantlie *The Sea our Heritage: British Maritime Interests Past and Present*. Keith, Banffshire: Rowan Books, 1995.

Thompson, Paul *Living the Fishing*. London: Routledge, 1983.

Tunstall, Jeremy *Fishermen: The Sociology of an Extreme Occupation*. MacGibbon and Kee (available through HarperCollins, London), 1962.

Ulyatt, Miacheal *Trawlermen of Hull: The Rise and Decline of the World's Greatest Fishing Port*. Skipton: Dalesman, 1985.

Waite, Renee *Sailing Past*. London: Seafarer, 1992.

Webb, William *Coastguard: An Official History of H.M. Coastguard*. London: HMSO, 1976.

Winton, John *For Those in Peril: Fifty Years of Royal Navy Search and Rescue*. London: Robert Hale, 1992.

Index

Numbers in bold type refer to the illustrations.

Index

Picture Credits

BBC Books would like to thank the following for providing photographs and for permission to reproduce copyright material. While every effort has been made to trace and acknowledge all copyright holders, we would like to apologise should there have been any errors or omissions.

Camera Press 49, 100, 108, 112, 131; John Frost Historical Newspapers 81, 161; Hulton Getty Picture Collection 2, 5, 15, 16, 20, 22/23, 24, 50, 51, 52, 73, 127, 128, 129, 155, 157, 158/159, 165; Illustrated London News 74; Imperial War Museum London 14, 71, 72, 77, 78, 80; Raymond Irons 6, 153; National Maritime Museum London 154; Popperfoto 9, 10/11, 26, 27, 105, 110/111, 162; Royal National Mission To Deep Sea Fishermen 55/56; Topham Picturepoint 19, 44, 47, 102/103, 106, 114, 132; Victoria and Albert Museum London 166.